PENSION GANGSTER

Pension Gangster

A No-Nonsense Guide to Ethical Pensions, Investments and Banking

TIM EWINS

RENARD PRESS

RENARD PRESS LTD

124 City Road
London EC1V 2NX
United Kingdom
info@renardpress.com
020 8050 2928

www.renardpress.com

Pension Gangster first published by Renard Press Ltd in 2025

Text © Tim Ewins, 2025
Illustrations © Beth Bridger, 2025
Cover design by Will Dady

Printed and bound in the UK on carbon-balanced papers by CMP Books

ISBN: 978-1-80447-143-2

9 8 7 6 5 4 3 2 1

Tim Ewins and Beth Bridger assert their moral right to be identified as the author and illustrator of this work respectively in accordance with the Copyright, Designs and Patents Act 1988.

The author believes information in this book given as facts to be correct at the time of writing, but feedback and corrections are welcome, and readers should do their own research rather than relying on this book. Companies have not been contacted for comment and are used for illustrative purposes only. Any links given have all been checked and accessed on the 5th of December 2024. The author and publishers cannot accept any liability for these websites and users should exercise caution and due diligence.

All rights reserved. This publication may not be reproduced, stored in a retrieval system or transmitted, in any form or by any means – electronic, mechanical, photocopying, recording or otherwise – without the prior permission of the publisher.

CLIMATE POSITIVE Renard Press is proud to be a climate positive publisher, removing more carbon from the air than we emit and planting a small forest. For more information see renardpress.com/eco.

The author withholds the right to identify as The Pension Gangster, having spent most his life livin' in a pension gangster's paradise.

EU Authorised Representative: Easy Access System Europe – Mustamäe tee 50, 10621 Tallinn, Estonia, gpsr.requests@easproject.com.

CONTENTS

Introduction: My wife, the pension gangster	11
• Important information before we get going	16
Chapter 1: What's the point?	18
• What's the point?	18
• What difference does it *really* make?	21
• *When* will we see a difference?	23
Chapter 2: Just a little bit of knowledge on the basics (pensions)	25
• Defined Contribution	30
- The structure of a Defined Contribution pension (and a KitKat)	31
- Product/pension provider	32
- Funds	34
- Company shares and other assets	35
- What can you do?	37
- The two subcategories of Defined Contribution pensions	38
• Workplace Pension	38
• Personal Pension	40
- Let's apply what we've learnt so far to Gemma… (includes the top ten holdings in the Aviva Managed fund)	40
• Defined Benefit	44
- What can you do?	46
- Let's apply what we've learnt so far to Gemma…	47

Chapter 3: Just a little bit of knowledge on the basics (regular, run-of-the-mill investments)	49
• The structure of a regular, run-of-the-mill investment	54
• What can you do?	57
• Let's apply what we've learnt so far to my six-year-old…	58
Chapter 4: Just a little bit of knowledge on the basics (banking)	61
• What can you do?	63
• Let's apply what we've learnt so far to me…	63
Chapter 5: What a conventional fund typically invests in	67
• The great pension swindle (includes the allocation of the top ten holdings in the Aviva Managed fund)	67
• A note on Nest	77
Chapter 6: The limited world of an ethical six-year-old (investments outside your pension)	84
Chapter 7: Supports, avoids, screening terms and 'other'	89
• Positive screening	90
• Negative screening	90
• Best in class	92
• Stewardship	92
Chapter 8: A brief foray into the sexy world of terminology	96
• ESG	96
• SRI	97
• Impact investing	97
• Light and dark green	97

Chapter 9: What an ethical fund typically invests in   99
(Includes the top ten holdings of the Aviva Stewardship
Managed fund, and the allocation of these holdings)

Chapter 10: Breaking myths   112
(like *Breaking Bad*, but better)
- Myth one: Ethical investments have not performed   112
  as well as traditional investments
- Myth two: Ethical investment is too young for us   115
  to fully understand
- Myth three: Ethical funds are risky   116
- Myth four: Ethical funds are more expensive   117

Chapter 11: Greenwashing   119
- Who is holding the funds and the fund managers   123
  themselves accountable?
  - The SFDR (the European one)   124
  - The SDR (the UK one)   124

Chapter 12: What you can do (pensions)   127
- Defined Contribution   128
  - Workplace Pensions   128
  - Personal Pensions   131
- Defined Benefit   135

Chapter 13: What you can do (regular,   137
run-of-the-mill investments)

Chapter 14: What you can do (banking)   141

Chapter 15: My wife, the pension goddess   144

Acknowledgements   149

PENSION GANGSTER

'I want you to write a non-fiction book next, Daddy.'

INDY (*aged six*)

INTRODUCTION

My wife, the pension gangster

My son invests his money globally, in several different asset classes and across a variety of companies and institutions. He's only six, though, so don't tell him or he'll want to buy some awful plastic toy with his money.

His mum, Gemma, and I save a small amount of money into an investment account each month on his behalf in the hope that it will grow – maybe not every year, but over the course of his childhood. One day, when he's old enough, we'll give him access to that money and he can buy all the plastic toys he wants. That'll be on him.

Gemma and I sat down one evening to discuss how we'd like his money to be invested, and from an ethical standpoint, we decided that we don't want our six-year-old to invest in:

- Gambling
- Tobacco
- Pornography or the sex industry
- Armaments

Now, he doesn't know what any of these things are, but I'd be willing to bet, based on who he is now, that eighteen-year-old him wouldn't want to be contributing to these industries. This might all sound rather simplistic, and it should be.

Most people wouldn't expect a six-year-old to be invested in tobacco or the sex industry, right? But many of them are.

Kids these days, eh?

~

With our son's future in mind, next we started to discuss our own investments. I'm going to level with you here: whilst I'm a financial adviser, I don't drive a Mercedes, and I live in a three-bed house on a nice but averagely priced estate. When we go on holiday, we use budget airlines or just set up a tent somewhere in Devon. We're not poor, but we're not rich, so, like most people, when I talk about my family's investments, I'm talking about our modest savings, bank accounts and pensions.

My pension was already invested in line with my own ethical preferences (I specialise in ethical investing, so frankly, if it wasn't, I'd be something of a hypocrite), but Gemma's pensions were like the Wild West. She was investing in alcohol, pornography, guns and tanks, pharmaceuticals, and all manner of fossil-fuel companies. Gemma was something of a pension gangster.

She has a pension that was set up by her previous employer, with a very large provider, invested in the default fund. When we looked at some of the companies the pension was invested in, Gemma felt uncomfortable, but it was her own fault. You see, here are the steps she took which led to having these questionable investments:

1. She got a job.
2. She... oh, wait.

That's all she did. She got a job, and I'm glad she did; we have bills to pay. Gemma's employer had, quite rightly, enrolled her into a company pension scheme in line with the Government's auto-enrolment rules, and she didn't opt out. And I'm glad she didn't opt out, because presumably we'll have bills to pay in retirement.

When the pension received a contribution from Gemma's first month's salary, her money was invested into the pension's default fund, and voilà, she became a pension gangster.

In short, Gemma was invested in these sectors, because, ultimately, she did nothing. Tut, tut, Gemma.

~

Then we started looking at our banking accounts. As it turns out, Gemma had already switched to the bank which best aligned with her ethical preferences. Me, however – well, I'm terrible.

You see, when I was sixteen, I opened a bank account. I grew up in a small UK seaside town with a choice of two banks and, naturally, I opened an account with the one nearest to my house, which was, of course, the same bank my parents used. I was very excited… I was given a chequebook! I'd become an adult.

That was in 2002, and up until very recently, I hadn't switched. Most people don't. Over the course of my lifetime (I'm thirty-eight), a current account hasn't offered much in the way of interest, and so there didn't feel like much point. The reward didn't seem to match up to the amount of admin and research involved.

This is a shame because, unfortunately, it's meant that for most of my life my cash savings have been funding the extraction of crude oil and I've been supporting, albeit inadvertently, a company with a huge gender pay gap. This is according to the bank's own report in 2020. I'm by no means saying I was banking with the worst, but it certainly wasn't the best.

I guess I'm no better than Gemma, then.

~

We're not unique. Unless you've actively made changes to your personal finances for ethical reasons, it is very likely that you're just like us. Most people – whether parents sensibly setting aside a pot for their children's future, members of a company pension, or just personal investors – have no idea where their money is invested or the impact it has on the world.

You might be spending your hard-earned money with an eco-aware mind. Maybe you favour cardboard over plastic and recycle religiously, or perhaps you brush your teeth with bamboo and car-share your electric vehicle – but have you taken the time to check your unspent money, by which I mean your savings, investments and/or pensions?

My family's money isn't going to radically affect the world, and, no offence, probably neither is yours, but when we pool our money together, and when we encourage our friends to do the same, and they encourage their friends, there is a small chance that we could make a difference.

So, how?

I mentioned earlier that I'm a financial adviser specialising in ethical investment. I help reasonably wealthy people invest their capital in accordance with their own ethical preferences. It's sad, but there is a certain level of capital typically required for a financial adviser to work with a client. It changes from adviser to adviser, but the reality is that the business model the industry favours is prohibitive for people with smaller amounts of wealth. This is commonly referred to as the advice gap. According to research conducted by the pension provider and life company Royal London in April 2021,[1] the average amount of savings an individual needs to hold before an adviser in the UK would consider taking them on as a client is £48,600.

If this is you, I would consider speaking with a financial adviser with a background in ethical investment.

If this isn't you, but you want to make sure that your capital is invested in a socially responsible and ethical manner, I'm sorry to say that the burden of research is likely to be on your shoulders. The industry is jargon heavy and opaque, and the default options are often 'conventional' (read: traditional and backwards facing).

That's why I'm writing this book. I want to help you fight through those initial barriers, understand the jargon and conquer the limitations. It should arm you with the right questions to ask and then empower you to make informed financial decisions and work out which are the right ones for you.

This book will:

- Explain what everything means and how to navigate the smokescreens;

---

[1] Royal London, *Exploring the Advice Gap* (April 2021). *https://adviser.royallondon.com/globalassets/docs/adviser/misc/br4pd0007-exploring-the-advice-gap-research-report.pdf*

- Show how to find out if your own finances are ethical or not;
- Show where to find investments and institutions which are more in line with your own personal ethical beliefs;
- Explain exactly how to make the changes you want to make.

~

Important information before we get going

A bit of housekeeping: I am a financial adviser, but I'm not going to be making any recommendations in this book. I will be mentioning specific products and investments, but purely to illustrate what I have found whilst conducting research for my family, not because I think you should do the same.

I don't know what your views are, and whilst I might mention some of mine along the way, I'm not for a second suggesting they're right – everyone's different.

Up until now, I've stuck inverted commas around the word 'conventional' when referring to what I consider to be a 'non-ethical' investment. This is because it isn't up to me to decide which investments are ethical, and the word 'conventional' doesn't necessarily mean 'normal', which is what it implies. For the sake of not overloading the pages of this book with inverted commas, from now on these will simply be called conventional investments. I might replace 'conventional' with 'traditional' from time to time, but in the same way that conventional doesn't necessarily mean normal, not all traditions are good. I make home-made mince pies every December, but are they better than the ones from the café down the road? I think we all know the answer

> to that. They take hours to make, and you can't bite into them when they're done.
>
> I'll keep bringing this next point up throughout the book, but on the off chance you intend to jump the gun, I'll say now that before making any changes to your personal savings, investments or pensions, you should make sure that you check past performance and financial standing carefully. Then you should make sure that you're making decisions which align with your own views on investment risk. Finally, at the risk of sounding like a broken record, impressive past performance of any investment fund does not guarantee future performance, and investments can go down as well as up – they really can. I've seen it and it's not pretty.
>
> This book is the journey of how I made my own family's finances more ethical, and it relays that journey in the hope that others might be inspired to do something similar. I've written what I've found, and then checked and double-checked my findings. Then I've cross-checked these findings with other industry professionals, but I can't guarantee 100% accuracy. I can guarantee 100% honesty, though, and 100% transparency on my behalf. If you contact me with questions, I will answer, and if you have any corrections, I'm all ears. You can be in touch via my website here:
>
> tim-ewins.com/contact

You may have read between the lines and noticed earlier in this chapter that Gemma and I were happy for our six-year-old to be invested in fossil fuels. There is a reason for this, and I can't wait to tell you what it is, so let's get started…

CHAPTER 1

What's the point?

You'll probably ask yourself (at least) two questions as you read this book:

1. What's the point?
2. What difference does it really make?

When it comes to your finances, a small change can make a big difference. A little adjustment to your pension, for example, can make a difference to the way the commercial world works – it can affect which companies garner market share and grow, and it can affect the future decisions of some of the world's largest multinationals.

I'd take it a step further and say that your personal finances are the single most important thing you can change in your life to make a real difference to the world, both environmentally and socially.

> *Making your pension green is 21x more powerful at cutting your carbon than giving up flying, going veggie and switching energy provider.*[1]

---

1 Make My Money Matter, *Is Your Pension Fuelling the Climate Crisis?* (2024). https://makemymoneymatter.co.uk/21x/

According to Make My Money Matter's research, changing to a greener pension has more impact than giving up flying, going veggie and switching energy provider – and they aren't just referring to one of these actions – it's combined.

When you make these changes to your finances, make no mistake, *personally* nothing will happen. You'll get a coffee and pat yourself on the back, but you probably won't deem it worthy of a celebratory meal out – probably not even a takeaway – but take it from me when I say you'll deserve one.

It'll be so underwhelming, in fact, that you'll probably start to ask yourself, What was the point? And what difference did you really make? Sometimes it can be hard to see through the smoke and carbon emissions, so I'll be as clear as possible.

What's the point?

You know when you go to the supermarket and they only have potatoes wrapped in plastic, but you *really* need potatoes so you buy them anyway because, come on, what difference will it make, really? Investment can be a bit like that. It's easier to find a conventional investment than it is an ethical one, and let's say you're investing £50 a month, it would be very easy to think, well, this is a drop in the ocean, it's not going to make a difference, and you'd probably be able to save yourself some time.

But then, what if everyone came together and refused to buy plastic-wrapped potatoes? The supermarkets would notice the unwrapped potatoes selling more, and eventually they'd stop selling the plastic-wrapped ones. I'm not saying that's going to happen, but I am saying that it *could* happen if enough people were to rebel.

For the record, I'm also not judging the people who buy plastic wrapped potatoes – imagine a roast dinner without potatoes – but I am judging the supermarkets for forcing their hand.

In the same way, if enough people place their money with ethically minded investment funds, other fund managers will take notice. Availability will increase, and new ethically minded funds with variations on different ethical criteria will pop up. We've already seen this happen over the last twenty years, and no matter what the value of your investment, you can help to continue that momentum.

And the change isn't even that big.

In the same way that a potato without plastic is still a potato, a fund without the questionable underlying investments is still a fund. It still aims to grow your capital in a competitive market, sensibly, and in a risk appropriate manner. Unless you invest directly in individual shares (which, if you follow this book, you won't), your hard-earned cash won't be directly funding small ethical start-ups or placed heavily in wind farms – not that that would be a bad thing, but for most people the risk would be too high.

When you look at the top ten companies an ethical fund invests in (which we will in Chapter 9), you'll mostly find huge corporations such as Apple, Mastercard and Microsoft. That might not be your idea of ethical (though, don't get me wrong, equally, it might be), and you may well point out that Apple, Mastercard and Microsoft all get investment from conventional investment funds as well as ethical investment funds.

You'd be right, which leads me nicely on to the next question…

What difference does it really make?

Companies want their shares to be held in ethical funds, but they also want their shares to be held in the more traditional funds. In fact, they want their shares to be held in any fund, because it raises the value of the shares and allows for greater growth.

Big companies whose shares were previously only eligible to be held in conventional funds are seeing average people like you and me invest our money into ethical funds, and they want a slice of the pie. The only way for them to get a slice of that pie is to improve their practices.

Sorry for calling you average – you're not. You're excellent.

The very fact that some of the world's biggest multinational conglomerates are appearing in the top ten holdings of most ethical funds shows that things are changing for the better. It's proof of progress. The bigger the companies showing up on these lists, the further the corporate world has progressed. We're aiming for a world where any company could be held in an ethical fund, and at that point, the goalposts can change.

The shares of less ethical companies can occasionally be found in certain ethical funds too, and this is because change can also be driven by fund managers exercising their shareholder rights to change the practices of these companies from within. We'll go into this properly in Chapter 7, but the same principle applies. The bigger the company, the bigger the overall impact.

So the individual decisions that we make with our money really can make a difference, provided others make similar decisions and changes.

Ethical investing isn't about ruining your pension, or about taking unnecessary risks. It certainly isn't virtue signalling. It's an effective and real way for the public to change corporate practices and hold companies accountable for their actions. It's about using your own money to better the planet, without even spending it.

The point I'm trying to make is that you can make a real difference. Just by making small adjustments to your current finances, you can set these mechanisms for change in motion and feed the machine. A small amount of your money can increase a fund-management company's power to influence a big company's decisions. These are the decisions that can make material difference to the future of our world.

It sounds over the top and dramatic, I know, but in answer to those questions, *that's* the point, and that's the difference it *really* makes.

~

I did get a bit passionate towards the end there. I felt like I was on a stage, and I got carried away, but I can't overemphasise how important this stuff is.

I own an 'ethical' bamboo toothbrush, and boy do I like to bang on about it at parties. But my toothbrush is going to do nothing in comparison to the way I invest my son's savings, or what I do with mine and Gemma's pensions. The toothbrush can't influence the biggest companies in the world, but my son's investments, and our pensions, can. Sadly, investments and pensions aren't sexy, so I can't talk about them too much because eventually I'll stop getting invited to parties.

I'm on thin ice with the toothbrush if I'm honest.

~

When will we see a difference?

The good news is that we're already seeing a difference. Twenty years ago, you'd have found it hard to find a basic ethical-investment fund offering competitive growth to its conventional counterparts. These days, whilst you might not be swimming in ethical opportunities, the market is much more competitive. There are hundreds of ethically minded funds to choose from, and there is usually an option to invest in at least one of these funds via your pension.

Don't forget that any investment, ethical or otherwise, is fundamentally an exercise in growing your money. Ethical investing isn't charity. If the performance wasn't matching up, we'd be moving in the wrong direction.

Thankfully, over the last decade, at least, this hasn't been the case, and the ethical arena continues to grow.

Global ESG assets are on track to exceed $53 trillion by 2025, representing more than a third of the $140.5 trillion in projected total assets under management.[1]

---

1 Bloomberg Professional Services, *ESG Assets May Hit $53 Trillion by 2025, a Third of Global AUM* (February 2021).
https://www.bloomberg.com/professional/blog/esg-assets-may-hit-53-trillion-by-2025-a-third-of-global-aum/

For ESG, by the way, read Ethical, Social and Governance. Bloomberg are referring to *global* assets under management, and if this pans out, it will be a huge deal. They specifically point out that growth in the market is being spurred by consumer demand (that's us – it's exactly what I've been talking about) and 'an unprecedented level of product development'. Product development refers to scientific developments, but make no mistake, scientific development is also driven by consumer demand, so that's also us.

See, didn't I say you weren't average.

~

Do you remember earlier in this chapter I was talking about plastic-wrapped potatoes, and how if enough people refused to buy them, eventually the supermarkets would stop bagging up their potatoes?

Well, you've probably noticed that most supermarkets have been selling loose potatoes for a while now. In fact, there are more loose bananas, broccoli, carrots, cauliflower, apples, mushrooms, baby sweetcorn, asparagus and avocados than there have been for years. This was a direct result of consumer demand, and the same can be said for ethical investing.

You're probably already investing in one way or another; possibly in a pension, maybe in an ISA (Individual Savings Account). You might simply be saving with a high-street bank.

I'm going to show you how to make sensible choices to ensure that your finances are as ethical as they can be, but to get to the good stuff, you'll need to come armed with just a little bit of knowledge on the basics. This is exactly what the next three chapters are going to offer, so I've named them…

CHAPTER 2

Just a little bit of knowledge on the basics (pensions)

Back in 2010, my then girlfriend Gemma (yep, *that* Gemma, the one with the gangster pension) moved to London. With no job or money, I followed her down from Nottingham. I know how it sounds, but I promise it was very romantic and not at all creepy. From my makeshift bed on the floor of my sister's London flat, I applied for any temp job going – customer care, waiting on tables and admin, all whilst performing amateur stand-up comedy in the evenings.

What a guy, right? That Gemma's a lucky lady.

Anyway, I needed cash, so when I was offered a three-week contract filing paperwork at a wealth-management firm in the city, I jumped at it.

Eight weeks into my three-week contract, I was approached by one of the directors.

'When does your contract end?' he asked.

'Um,' I replied, feeling caught out. It was time to fess up. 'It ended five weeks ago, but I kept coming because you kept paying me.' I sighed, defeated. I was going to be out of a job by the end of the day.

'That shows initiative,' the director replied. 'How would you like to join the graduate programme?' The following week, I was sitting at a computer, trying to complete the entry-level tests.

Here are some of the words and terms that, by that point in my life, I had never heard of:

- ISA
- Compound interest
- Pension benefits
- Fund
- Collective investment
- Gross
- Net

Reader, I did not pass that test.

I did make a damn fine cup of tea, though, so I was allowed to file for a few more weeks before taking it again.

I was a graduate, and by that standard, I was allowed on the graduate scheme, but I was a graduate of English and Performing Arts, not business or finance, so I had a lot of learning ahead of me.

The next three chapters might come across as a little patronising, and you may already know and understand everything in them, but I certainly wouldn't have back in 2010. I think there are a lot of people like 2010 me, which is a shame, because everyone should know the basics when it comes to saving, investing and planning for retirement. It's a basic life skill, and the fact that people don't is a failing of the education system – but that's a whole other book.

Just to put your mind at ease, I did pass that test the second time around before signing up to the graduate scheme. I wasn't as productive as my colleagues, though, because I still had to do the filing and make the drinks. I guess that's the price of making a damn fine cup of tea.

It's been over a decade since I took that test, and now I'm someone who not only understands pensions and investments, but I also find them interesting – occasionally even exciting. Gemma doesn't think they can be. Over this and the next chapter, I'm going to prove her wrong...

~

There are hundreds of different types of pensions, and it's easy to get bogged down in the technical information. You'll probably receive a statement each year, and that's likely to come with several pages of confusing explanation. On the first page of the statement, it will likely (but annoyingly, not always) state the type of pension you hold. This could say Stakeholder, SIPP, Workplace Pension, SSAS, Section 32, Final Salary, Scheme Pension, Personal Pension... The list goes on, and on, and on.

All these terms have specific meanings: some can invest in assets that others can't; some have caps on the maximum fees which can be charged; and others simply refer to historic legislation. Sometimes this legislation isn't even relevant any more. It's an absolute minefield.

Then, as if that wasn't enough, most providers (the company with whom you hold your pension) have given additional names to their products. Sometimes, instead of stating 'SIPP', for example (which stands for Self-Invested Personal Pension, if you're wondering), the statement could say something like 'Your Retirement

Plan 7'. This suggests that you have six other retirement plans with this provider, but you don't — or I suppose you might, but this isn't what the seven refers to. No, to decipher what the name means, you'd have to go to the provider's website, navigate to the relevant product and dive deep into their descriptions.

Even I'm with Gemma up to this point — nothing I've said is exciting.

So far, I've only talked about the first few words on a pension statement, so it's no wonder these painfully long documents spend so much time on the kitchen side and end up at the back of a cupboard.

The world of pensions is confusing, and it shouldn't be, because most of us have one. To help you understand how your pension either is, or isn't, ethical, first I'm going to have to over-simplify here, and say that all pensions can be placed into one of two categories, with one of the categories falling into two subcategories.

I've created a 'what type of pension have you got quiz?' below, so you can skip to the relevant section of the book for you. It's in the style of one of those 'Which Spice Girl Are You?' type quizzes, so I feel like I'm already proving to Gemma that pensions can be fun, if not yet exciting.

I was Baby Spice, by the way. Always Baby. I wanted to be Scary, just once.

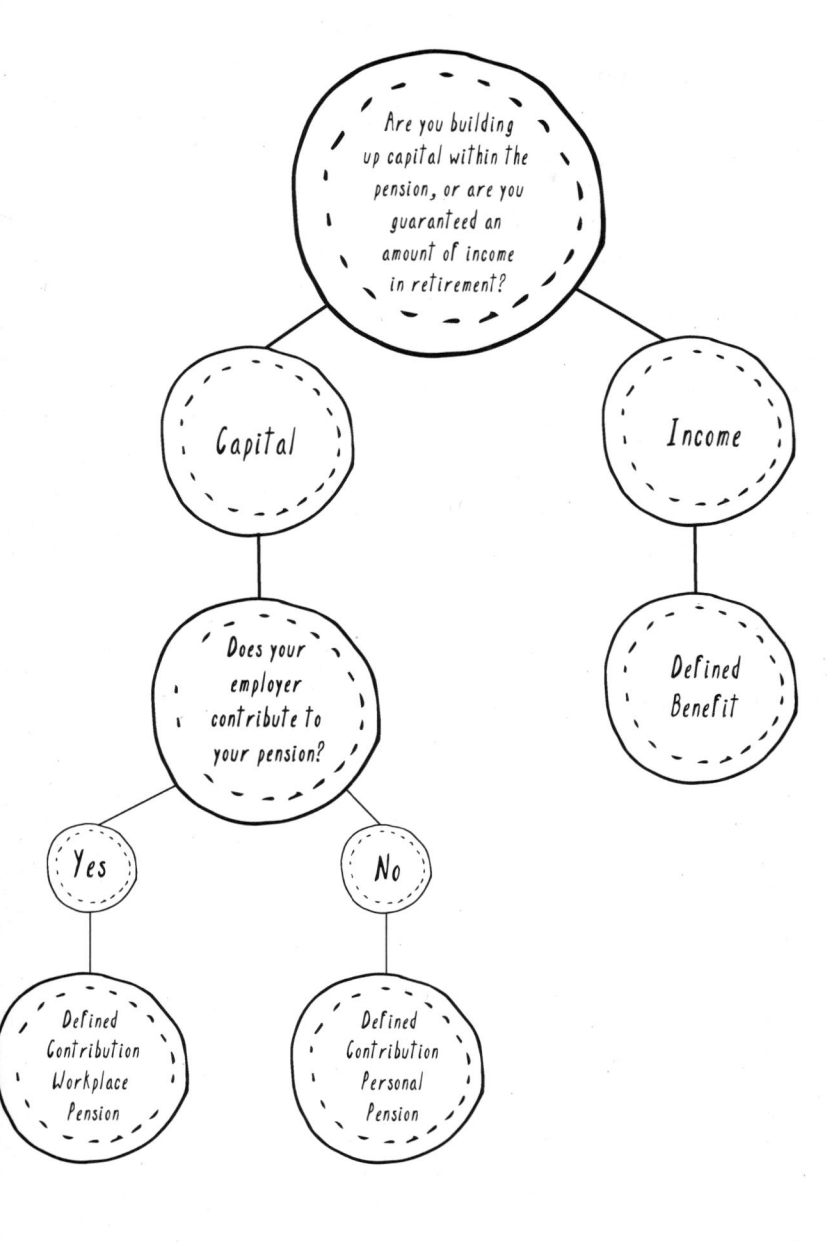

Defined Contribution

You might also know these as 'Money Purchase' pensions.

In simple terms, a Defined Contribution pension is a sum of money held inside an account with specific tax rules. You, or your employer, pay money into the pension, and that money is invested until you retire, and often long after that. There are no guarantees in a Defined Contribution pension.

Let's say you hold a Defined Contribution pension, and you receive a statement which tells you it has a value of £2,000. Your £2,000 should be (and in most cases, will be) invested in the hope that it grows before you retire. Because it's invested, tomorrow it could be worth more or less than what it says on the statement, depending on whether your investment has gained or lost value overnight, but that doesn't matter. Your pension is going to stay invested until you take money out of it, which is likely to be when you retire. Provided the overall value goes up before then, it's fine for it to fluctuate every day.

If you do receive a Defined Contribution pension statement with a value of £2,000, fear not. You are not alone. There are millions of us with small pensions, and at retirement we can form a commune or something – I honestly don't know what the plan is, that'll be for a future Government to work out, but if they come up with nothing, a commune might at least be fun.

Anyway, these pensions are called 'Defined Contribution' pensions because the benefit you receive is equal to the contribution made into it, plus whatever growth it might achieve, minus the pension fees. The contribution can quite literally be defined, either by yourself, or your employer, or both.

THE BASICS (PENSIONS)

If you contribute £2,000 gross (i.e. including the tax relief) into a Defined Contribution pension, and the investment grows by £500 over the course of your working life, at retirement you would get a benefit of £2,500 (excluding fees).

To be absolutely clear, this is £2,500 in total, *not* £2,500 each year, as some people hope and believe it to be. If you take it out and spend it, it's gone.

But don't worry, if we start a commune, we can grow our own food.

The structure of a Defined Contribution pension (and a KitKat)

In basic terms, Defined Contribution pensions are structured as follows:

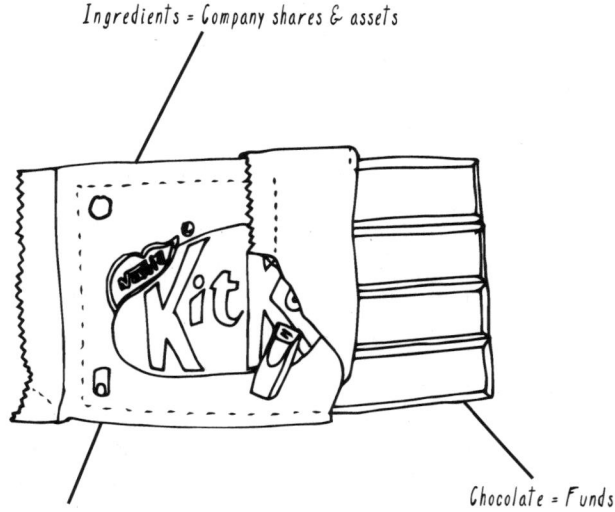

Ingredients = Company shares & assets

Chocolate = Funds

Wrapper = Product or Pension Provider

Most Defined Contribution pensions consist of a fund, or funds, that hold shares in a collection of companies or other assets. This fund, or these funds, are held with a product provider.

But clearly, Beth Bridger (the fine illustrator of the above) has drawn a KitKat.

That is because, if a Defined Contribution pension was a KitKat, the shares in companies would be the ingredients, the fund (or funds) would be the chocolate bar holding the ingredients together, and the product provider providing the pension wrapper would be Nestlé providing a literal wrapper in which to hold the chocolate bar.

And if that's the last time we mention Nestlé in this book about ethics, they'll have got off very lightly.

Let's take a look at each level in more detail, starting at the top level – the product provider/KitKat wrapper.

Product/pension provider

This refers to the company which looks after your pension, and in the previous analogy, it's the KitKat wrapper. Here are some of the most common providers:

- Aegon
- Aviva
- AXA
- Canada Life
- Fidelity
- Friends Life
- Legal and General
- Nest
- Phoenix Life
- Prudential
- Royal London
- Scottish Widows
- Scottish Life
- Scottish Widows
- Standard Life
- Zurich

This is not an exhaustive list, but these are the providers which come up most in my day-to-day work.

It's a common misconception that product providers are the driver behind whether a Defined Contribution pension performs well or not. If you hold an Aegon Defined Contribution pension, for example, and you see that it's gone down in value, it's not necessarily Aegon's fault. Aegon is merely holding the fund for you, and it's the fund, along with the shares and other assets which the fund invests in, which drive the performance (or lack of).

If a KitKat goes out of date (i.e. performs badly), no one blames the wrapper unless it's broken – it's the longevity of the chocolate and the ingredients themselves that have failed over time. The wrapper is just packaging for the chocolate and the ingredients.

And not that this is relevant to the pension analogy, but I'd probably still eat that KitKat.

In fact, going back to pensions, unless it's invested in one of the providers' own funds, it isn't even the provider that holds your money, it's the fund itself. So, whilst I'm sure there are both ethical and non-ethical practices at this level, for the most part I'm not going to focus on the product provider. This isn't where your money is being invested. All we need at this level is for providers to offer the right funds, and then to shout about it.

If Nestlé were to change KitKat's ingredients to be sustainable and natural, I'm sure they'd shout about it. I imagine it would be quite hard for Nestlé to successfully do that, because it wouldn't taste the same, but it isn't hard for pension providers to offer better funds, because they are available, people want them, and no one's eating their pension.

Funds

In this chocolatey analogy, the bar inside the wrapper is the pension fund. If you've never made an effort with your Defined Contribution pension, your money will most likely be invested in just one fund.

Assuming your employer set your pension up for you, and assuming you haven't personally made any changes, your money will be invested into the default fund. This means that not only is your money in one fund, but you didn't even choose that fund.

These funds tend to be 'balanced managed' funds, which translates to a 'balanced' level of investment risk, and 'managed' by a fund manager. The 'managed' part is irrelevant really, because most, if not all, UK regulated funds have fund managers and are managed in one way or another.

You know how KitKats have 'KitKat' engraved into the chocolate on each finger? Well, the word KitKat is nothing more than marketing. It doesn't describe what the chocolate bar is actually made of. If it did, I think less people would eat KitKats. In the same way, 'balanced managed' doesn't explain how your money is really invested. It doesn't go into the ingredients of the fund.

These default funds have been selected to be a catch-all for people who aren't interested in – or don't have the time to make changes to – their pension, and so the result is tens of millions of people who are invested in the same funds. The intention is presumably good, and it solves the problem of an understandably disengaged population, but that doesn't mean that it's the right fund for you.

In the UK, 49.4% of a KitKat is sugar,[1] and it gets worse the deeper into the ingredients list you delve. No one's really checking, though, so it's easy to ignore.

That's how default funds work too.

When you consider the sheer amount of people investing their whole pension into these same funds, it becomes clear that we're placing *very* large collective amounts of money with certain companies, and the customers (that's you and I) aren't checking which ones. The question you need to ask is: are these the companies which *you* feel comfortable investing in?

You might also want to ask yourself whether you really *need* that KitKat…

Company shares and other assets

One ingredient does not make a KitKat, and one company share does not make a fund. You won't be surprised to hear that Nestlé are not the only chocolate manufacturer using sugar, but their recipes, when including other ingredients, are unique to them. A typical 'balanced managed' fund will typically hold shares in over a hundred companies (along with other asset types, which we can talk about later), and it's this combination of shares and holdings that makes the fund unique.

There is a very good reason why funds have to work this way, and it's in your interest that they do.

Let's take AstraZeneca (the COVID vaccine guys) for example. Most default UK pension funds will hold shares

---

1   https://www.kitkat.co.uk/products/finger-milk-chocolate

in AstraZeneca. It's one of the top FTSE 100 companies, and has historically offered a strong return. But that doesn't mean you'd want all your pension – all your *retirement* – to be reliant on AstraZeneca. What if AstraZeneca share prices fell dramatically – or worse yet, the company became insolvent? It could seriously affect your pension, and, ultimately, your life. To save this from happening, fund managers will invest in the shares of lots of other companies too.

If one share price falls, or a company goes under, the fund will only be partially affected, as only a small percentage of the fund will be invested with that company. It diversifies the fund, and it mitigates the risk.

On an individual level for each investor (that's us again), this makes the holding feel insignificant. It's such a tiny amount of our own personal money, but don't forget the millions of other people invested in the same fund. Collectively, we're enabling the fund manager to invest an astronomical amount of money with each company they choose to invest in.

But wait… all this aside, what if you don't want to invest in AstraZeneca? What if you don't feel comfortable investing in pharmaceuticals at all? What can you do? Well, you can't take one company out of a fund, but you can switch to a different fund that doesn't hold any shares in that company.

There is a kicker here, though. The difference between a KitKat and a fund is that Nestlé are required to list all their ingredients, whereas a fund manager only has to list the top ten holdings of their fund. The rest is considered their intellectual property.

So, whilst you can pick a fund that doesn't have AstraZeneca as one of its top ten holdings, AstraZeneca could well be holding number eleven.

THE BASICS (PENSIONS)

Realistically, unless you have a huge pension and incredible levels of investment experience, you're not going to be able to directly buy the necessary amount of individual shares required to create a sensible retirement portfolio, let alone one that specifically aligns to your ethical criteria. Even if you did possess these qualities, most Defined Contribution product providers wouldn't even allow you to buy the necessary individual shares.

You wouldn't try to make a KitKat from scratch, so don't try to make a fund.

We are stuck with the current system, so how can you better your Defined Contribution pension?

What can you do?

Like I say, you probably wouldn't try to create a KitKat from scratch, but if you didn't like one of the ingredients, you could choose to buy a Freddo.[1]

If you can't pick the companies your pension invests in directly (and as we've just seen, you probably can't), you need to focus on the fund/chocolate bar level.

Which fund fits most closely to your personal ethical views? There are ways to find out, and we'll go through them properly in Chapters 7 and 8.

If, when you've researched the funds that are available in your pension, you find that none of them fit with how you'd like your pension to be invested, this is the point at which you need to

---

[1] I haven't actually compared the ingredients list of a KitKat and a Freddo, but they can't be the same. For starters, one presumably includes frog.

focus on the product provider level. Remember, the product provider is just the wrapper — they don't hold or invest your money, but different product providers offer different funds.

Maybe you're not interested in KitKats at all — not a Chunky, or even a Chunky Peanut Butter. This is how you find your Freddo.

Just like buying a different wrapper at the supermarket will give you a different bar of chocolate, changing your pension product provider could open up your fund options.

It sounds complicated, but it doesn't have to be, and I'm here to help.

The two subcategories of Defined Contribution pensions

Broadly speaking there are two types of Defined Contribution pension:

1. Workplace Pension

This is a pension that is set up by your employer. There are lots of different types of, and terms for, a Workplace Pension (Stakeholder, Scheme Pension, Group Personal Pension), but Defined Contribution Workplace Pensions all follow the KitKat structure we've just looked at.

In 2012, employers were legislatively required to enrol eligible employees into a Workplace Pension. If you're earning over £10,000 and you're aged over twenty-two but below the State Pension age, you'll probably have one.

Let's just take a second to consider how many people in the UK fall into this bracket, and how many of them take an active interest in their pension. That's a lot of people's

THE BASICS (PENSIONS)

money being unknowingly directed into a relatively small number of companies.

If you have a Defined Contribution Workplace Pension, it's likely you'll be making monthly contributions *from* your salary, and your employer will be making monthly contributions *on top of* your salary. This is important, and it's why you don't want to move your Defined Contribution Workplace Pension. Those contributions from your employer are free money.

Unless you've taken an active interest in your pension already, though, these contributions will be getting invested into a fund which you haven't picked yourself. There is a very high chance that your pension will be invested in alcohol, pornography, guns and tanks, pharmaceuticals, deforestation and all manner of fossil-fuel companies.

This is how Gemma became a pension gangster, and it's why you're probably a straight-up G too (a straight-up Pension G, that is).

In most cases, Defined Contribution Workplace Pensions can't be moved to a different product provider without losing that lovely free money you're getting from your employer, so if you can't find a fund that fits your ethical preferences within the existing pension, you probably still wouldn't want to move it. I know, it's not ideal, but it's not quite 'pension gangster till I die' territory yet – we'll look at what you *can* do soon.

If you have a Defined Contribution Workplace Pension from an old employer, with no contributions going in any more, you'll be able to research not only the funds you want to invest in, but also the product providers that offer the funds you're interested in too.

There's hope for you yet, G. Get yourself out of the game. You're better than this.

2. Personal Pension

If you have one of these, you probably set it up yourself. You might be making regular contributions, or you might not be. You'll probably have more choice of funds in this pension than in a Defined Contribution Workplace Pension, but not necessarily. If the fund choice is limited and you can't find the right fund for you, you'll probably (though not always) be able to move it to a different product provider.

That doesn't mean a Personal Pension is better because, remember, you're not getting that lovely free money from your employer. You might find it easier to get out of the game, but you were never rolling in the dough when you were in it.

Let's apply what we've learnt so far to Gemma...

Gemma, aka the Original Pension Gangster (OPG), has an Aviva pension. Aviva is the product provider.

Gemma is invested in the Aviva Managed fund (which fits perfectly into the 'balanced managed' category – see the 'funds' section of this chapter on p. 34), and her pension has thirty funds to choose from, including the one she's invested in. This is actually pretty good for a Workplace Pension.

Gemma's pension is a classic KitKat. It has a nice wrapper, and the chocolate bar inside is nicely branded. I wonder what the ingredients are...

It's hard to know because, as we've already seen, fund managers only publish their top ten holdings. Most funds invest in over a hundred companies, meaning there is a huge amount of information not available to the public about how their money is being invested.

Let's work with what we've got, and take a look at what the top ten holdings in the Aviva Managed fund are (at the time of writing):[1]

- 3.8% in *US Treasury 1.123% Index-Linked 01/33*: This isn't a company, it's a US Government bond.
- 1.9% in *Microsoft Corporation*: I know you already know about Microsoft, but if I'm going to clarify some, I'm going to have to clarify them all. So Microsoft is a multinational tech company. Let's play a game with this: the holding after the next one is called *Apple* – see if you can guess which one.
- 1.5% in *SPDR ETF Bloomberg Emerging Markets Local Bonds UCITS*: This is a more specialised fund, held inside the Aviva Managed fund. The fund manager is aiming to track the debt of emerging markets (the economies of developing countries). Like the Aviva Managed fund, this fund will have underlying holdings, only the top ten of which will be disclosed. I won't delve into what they are, because no investor would. Talk about smoke and mirrors.

---

[1] I would love to add a link to the Factsheet/KIID here, but each time the document is updated the previous one is removed from the public domain, so any link would become obsolete quickly. Due to falling interest rates, the latest list holds a higher percentage in bonds and gilts, which are much less fun to write or read about than company shares. I've used the most up-to-date information available, which reflects the fund under 'normal' market conditions.

- 1.4% in *Apple*: If you guessed the record label founded by The Beatles in 1968, sadly you were wrong. This refers to Apple, the multinational tech company. Also, if you guessed the fruit, again, sadly not.
- 1.2% in *UK Treasury Bill 0% 11/12/2023*: Like number one, this isn't a company, but rather a UK Treasury Bill which has been issued by the UK Government.
- 0.9% in *AstraZeneca*: I mentioned these folks earlier, but they're a multinational pharmaceutical and biotechnology company. AstraZeneca was a pretty big deal towards the end of COVID-19, so most people now know about it, even if it's just as something they used to have to stick in their arm before they went on holiday.
- 0.9% in *Alphabet Incorporated*: A multinational tech conglomerate which was created through a restructuring of Google. So, essentially, this is sort of Google.
- 0.8% in *Shell*: A multinational oil and gas company. Hey, I wonder if they'll show up on Aviva's ethical counterpart to this fund...
- 0.7% in *Amazon.com*: A multinational tech and e-commerce company. You know, the really big online shop – a bit like how round the back of Argos was back in the day, but bigger.
- 0.7% in *Nestlé S.A.*: A multinational food and drink processing conglomerate. These guys make KitKats, so they *must* be good, right? I mean, just look at the wrappers – they're so shiny.

These holdings probably won't come as a huge shock to you. It's a mix of some of the biggest companies in the world, with a couple of Government bonds thrown in to reduce the overall risk of the fund.

I don't think I'm speaking out of turn here when I say Shell and Nestlé don't have the best track record when it comes to their ethical practices, and actually, hasn't Amazon.com had some bad press around workers' rights, tax avoidance and its environmental impact?

Yes. Yes, it has.

Look, I'm not here to judge. I'll have to sell this book somewhere.

It'll be interesting which of these companies show up when we look at the fund Gemma moves into later in the book, but also, these are only the top ten holdings. It discloses only 13.8% of the overall fund. Where is the other 86.2% of Gemma's pension invested?

There is no way to find out.

With the right software, though, it is possible to place filters on the fund to at least see what sectors might be hiding under there, but we'll get to that later on in the book.

In theory, Gemma has chosen this fund. Except, of course, she hasn't, and because she hasn't, her then employer chose one for her (and most of her colleagues). Her then employer was given thirty funds to choose from, and because her then employer was making decisions for other people they've chosen the most bog-standard fund available. Any fund claiming to be 'sustainable' or 'ethical' could be seen as being a little left field, and who are they to make those kinds of decisions for Gemma?

As far as they see it, conventional = normal, remember? Traditional = good (honestly, my home-made mince pies aren't that bad, and I'd know, because I'm the only one who eats them).

To take control of her pension and break free from her gangster life, Gemma will look at the thirty funds available to her, because maybe the right one for her is in that list. If this was a Workplace Pension which was still receiving employer contributions from her employer, Gemma would likely have to pick one of the thirty, but she's recently gone freelance, so now there aren't any contributions going in. This means she can probably transfer the pension to a different product provider if she needs to, so she can get the right fund for her.

As a side note, I'll be using the Aviva Managed fund throughout this book, analysing the underlying holdings to see how it stacks up against different ethical criteria. I'm only using this fund as an example, and it's been chosen because it is genuinely what Gemma's pension is invested in. I've not contacted Aviva, and have no affiliation with them, but the Aviva Managed fund will invest very similarly to most other balanced managed/conventional funds on the market.

It doesn't claim to be an ethical fund, so let's not be giving it any lip.

Defined Benefit

The second category of pension we're going to look at is Defined Benefit, which you might also know as 'Final Salary' or 'Career Average' pensions. Unlike a Defined Contribution pension, a Defined Benefit pension offers a guaranteed income for life at retirement, but it doesn't have a capital value specifically allocated to you.

Similar to a Defined Contribution pension, you and your employer might both contribute money to the Defined Benefit scheme each month, but rather than seeing that money appear in an account, you'll see the income you can expect to receive in retirement increase.

Let's say you hold a Defined Benefit pension, and you receive a statement that tells you it has a benefit of £2,000. This means that at retirement you will receive (at least) £2,000 per annum, which is likely to increase each year with inflation. You might be offered to swap some of this income for a lump sum.

Do you remember the commune we were discussing in the Defined Contribution section of this chapter? Well, if you have a reasonable Defined Benefit pension (read, *more* than £2,000 a year), you might not be invited into the fold, but that's ok. You'll be dining on Sainsbury's Taste the Difference prawns whilst the rest of us are scrambling for home-grown carrots in borrowed land.

A Defined Benefit pension will have an amount of money behind the scenes, which will be managed by the scheme trustees. This is the money which is used to fund the retirement of members who have already retired, and, one day, it will be used to fund your retirement. This money is invested by the trustees, and, just like a Defined Contribution pension, tomorrow it could be worth more or less than it's worth today. This time it *really* doesn't matter, because what you receive at retirement does not change at all. The responsibility of paying this guaranteed income is on the scheme, not on you. If the fund falls, you will still receive the same level of income, because the risk is held by the scheme itself.[1]

---

[1] If the scheme is being wound up and cannot pay benefits, the Pension Protection Fund (a Government-sponsored fund) will pay compensation close to, if not equal to, the benefits.

What can you do?

Sadly, you don't have much say in the behind-the-scenes investing of your Defined Benefit pension, and it's not like a KitKat – you can't just choose to get a Freddo instead, and you can't easily change the ingredients. It isn't up to you, and the stakes are just too high for the scheme. All liability lies with them, and so the responsibility is also with them. There isn't a specific amount of money designated to you, personally, so any changes made would be made on behalf of every person in the pension scheme.[1]

There are very few Defined Benefit pensions that have an ethical statement or criteria, but a small number of them do. You can request one from your scheme, but if they don't have one, prepare for the person on the other end of the phone to be confused.

If your Defined Benefit pension doesn't have an ethical statement, or if it does but it doesn't match up to your expectations, there is very little that can be done about it. For that reason, this book will skip on Defined Benefit pensions for the most part, though we will briefly revisit that teeny tiny area which might make a difference in Chapter 12.

---

1 It is sometimes possible to transfer your Defined Benefit pension into a Defined Contribution pension and then you could choose which fund your capital is invested in, but it's very rare that it would be in your best interest to do so. If that is something you're considering, you should seek regulated advice (at the time of writing, if your transfer value is above £30,000 the scheme would refuse to transfer it without you having sought advice first).

Let's apply what we've learnt so far to Gemma...

I've discussed Defined Benefit pensions because if you have one but don't know the difference between a Defined Benefit and a Defined Contribution pension, you could end up reading this whole book and then applying the Defined Contribution rules to your Defined Benefit pension. You'd end up confused, and so would some poor administrator at the pension scheme. Then you'd probably give this book a bad review (don't), and who knows, maybe so would the administrator (tell them not to).

There's one other slight deviation from the type of Defined Benefit pension we've just been talking about, which, thankfully, Gemma's employment history can illustrate quite nicely.

Gemma was a teacher for five years before she moved back to marketing. During that time, she was a member of the Teachers' Pension, and one day, when she retires, this pension will become a guaranteed income.

Classic Defined Benefit.

Whilst it's not a very big income, it's still a valuable thing to have, because it equates to about one takeaway pizza every month throughout her retirement (it's cool, we can share).

However, Gemma won't be looking for an ethical statement from her Defined Benefit pension, nor will she be calling them about the underlying investments.

The Teacher's Pension, like the Firefighters' Pension, Armed Forces Pension, NHS Pension and many local government pensions, is unfunded. This means that there isn't a central fund, and so there is no specific underlying investment. The benefits of these pensions are paid solely by the taxpayer, and so there really isn't anything you (or Gemma) can do to change them, aside from writing a letter to the Government.

Don't beat yourself up about it, though, if you have one of these pensions – you've probably already done a smashing job for the community and helped a lot of people in the mean time, so thank you. Grab yourself a cuppa and give yourself a pat on the back.

CHAPTER 3

Just a little bit of knowledge on the basics (regular, run-of-the-mill investments)

By which I mean your own personal investments – the ones not held inside a pension – and for most people in the UK, the ones that don't exist. I'm not talking about cash ISAs or savings accounts with your bank. I'm talking about stocks and shares ISAs or investments which go up and down in value.

For my family, these investments do exist, but they're earmarked for the kiddo, so I don't feel all that fancy about it.

The structure of these investments is the same as with Defined Contribution pensions (the KitKats analogy), but the obstacles are slightly different. Pensions are one of the more complex areas of finance, so you'd expect this section to be a little lighter going than the last, but here's the thing – most pensions only offer a few funds. Whilst this can be limiting, and often means that you won't be able to achieve what you'd like to from an ethical standpoint in your pension, it does also mean there is less research to be done, at least when it comes to picking a fund.

The best platforms for investment outside of a pension offer *every* UK regulated fund on the market. Many of them also allow you to invest into individual companies, skipping the KitKat bar (the fund itself) step of the process completely, jumping straight into the ingredients (the company shares). If you wanted to, you could create your own chocolate bar, metaphorically speaking. This sounds freeing, but it can also be daunting.

~

I should clarify what I mean by 'regular, run-of-the-mill investments'.

I don't mean cash.

Cash offers a rate of return via interest and, whilst it might lose its real value over time (because of inflation), it won't literally fall in value. If you hold £100 in a cash account with no interest rate for a year, next year you will still hold £100.

Regular, run-of-the-mill investments will drop in value from time to time, and increase in value from time to time. Sometimes these investments will drop in value considerably for a long period of time, and because of my job, I'm trained to really hammer that point home... I wouldn't feel comfortable if I didn't also do that here, so here goes:

You could invest £100 and after a year it could be worth £80, which doesn't sound too bad, but investment is measured by percentage, so that's the same as investing £10,000 and after a year having only £8,000. Boom – you've lost £2,000 in a year. It doesn't look nice on paper, but believe me, it feels much worse when it's your own hard-earned money.

I've watched my son's investments drop considerably twice over his little lifetime (COVID and the cost-of-living crisis), and even though I understand why, and even though I know he's going to continue investing this money until he's at least

THE BASICS (REGULAR, RUN-OF-THE-MILL INVESTMENTS)

eighteen, it still doesn't feel good. I'm not saying this to put you off investing, I'm saying it to emphasise the importance of investing sensibly, and for a long time. I'm also saying it to prepare you.

Investments do tend to go up as well, and historically, more often than down. The US Stock Market Index, the Standard & Poor's 500 (S&P 500)[1], has had overall losses in ten out of the fifty years between 1974 and 2024. The other forty years have shown gains.[2] This emphasises the importance of investing for a long time. If you only invest for one year, it could well be one of those years where the market falls. If you invest for two years, it could be that the market falls for two consecutive years, or that the year of growth doesn't make up for the fall in the other year. If you invest for three years, there isn't any guarantee that you'll end up with more money than you started with, but statistically speaking it becomes probable. The longer you invest, the more likely you are to grow your money and not lose out overall. To put that into practice, here's what my family are up to with our money:

We want to convert our loft so that we have a spare bedroom for family and friends to stay in when they come over. Selfishly, our loved ones live all over the country. I know, right? Hopefully, we'll convert the loft in the next year or two. We save this money into a high-interest cash account,

---

1 The S&P specifically refers to the 500 largest listed companies in the US, so it doesn't necessarily reflect a well-spread investment, but is being used here to illustrate the point.

2 Aswath Damodaran, 'Historical Returns on Stocks, Bonds and Bills: 1928–2024' (January 2025).
https://pages.stern.nyu.edu/~adamodar/New_Home_Page/datafile/histretSP.html

and whilst it's unlikely to keep up with inflation, if the market drops when we start work on the loft, our savings won't have dropped with it.

To be clear, we'll need this money soon, so we haven't invested it. It won't fall if the market falls.

Because of inflation, the loft conversion might cost more by the time we get around to it. Mind you, because of procrastination and my childish desire to buy a robot lawnmower, it might never happen anyway – but let's not tell Gemma that.

We also save £100 into my six-year-old's investment account every month. This is the money which we do invest, and that is because we know he won't be able to spend it until he's at least eighteen. That's a time-horizon of twelve years, so the odds are that the value of his investments will go up. There are likely to be more positive years than negative. There's no guarantee, but it's certainly likely.

The reason I've referred to investments here as being 'regular' and 'run of the mill' is because that's what we're primarily going to be looking at. As I've already mentioned, the best platforms for investment allow you to invest in anything regulated by the Financial Conduct Authority (FCA), assuming you're reading this in the UK. I'm going to assume you don't want to invest in individual shares, or anything very risky.

I'm also going to assume that you're looking to invest an amount lower than £48,600 (over which amount, as we've already discussed, you might benefit from financial advice).

A sensible way to invest over a long period of time is to hold small portions of your money in different asset

THE BASICS (REGULAR, RUN-OF-THE-MILL INVESTMENTS)

classes. This simply refers to whether the money is held in companies (equities), bonds (be they corporate or government), property (normally commercial) or commodities (such as gold). I'm not going to go into the different asset classes as there is so much information out there already,[1] but I will say that a way to bypass having to focus on this is to put your money with a fund that invests across all, or several asset classes. These funds are called multi-asset funds.

The information provided by the multi-asset fund itself should tell you how much investment risk it takes, and that's ultimately what the allocation to each asset class pertains to. You want it a little riskier? You add a higher proportion of equity holdings and shares. You want to lower the risk? You add in a few more bonds and money market holdings.

Most multi-asset funds are what I would consider to be regular, run-of-the-mill investments.

Finally, whilst there is often less choice in a pension, the Defined Contribution pensions which we looked at in the last chapter often invest in similar multi-asset funds (think – balanced managed), so there will be some crossover here…

---

[1] A straightforward breakdown provided by investment management firm Schroders can be found here: 'Asset Classes Explained: A Quick Guide to Building a Diversified Portfolio' (July 2023). https://www.schroders.com/en-gb/uk/individual/content/asset-classes-explained-a-quick-guide-to-building-a-diversified-portfolio/

The structure of a regular, run-of-the-mill investment

A regular, run-of-the-mill investment is structured in a very similar way to the structure of a Defined Contribution pension, and indeed, you guessed it, a KitKat:

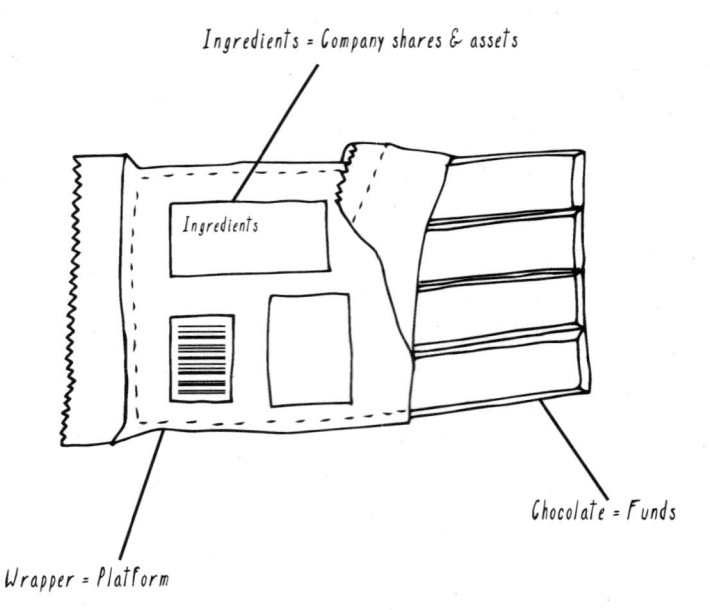

Ingredients = Company shares & assets

Chocolate = Funds

Wrapper = Platform

The structure is so similar to a Defined Contribution pension, in fact, that I won't patronise you by going through it again here. The product provider level here is referred to as the platform, but it's the same concept.

Assuming you're investing a relatively small sum of money (remember the £48,600 rule), and assuming you don't have a huge amount of investment experience, you'll probably want to invest in a multi-asset fund.

The biggest difference between making a direct investment and making an investment in a Defined Contribution pension is that you'll usually be given more choice of where to invest your money, and you'll have to make all the decisions yourself. Assuming you research funds before you find a platform, you'll have several thousand funds to choose from. There won't be a default fund either, so you're starting from scratch.

This can be a lot to get your head around, and I know people who have put off investing their money for years because it feels too much. They worry that they'll pick the wrong fund, they don't know how to research any of the thousands of investments on offer, and then, understandably, they give up.

To make sure you don't fall into this trap, the three basic components you need to check are:

1. Risk
2. Performance
3. Fees

You can find the risk level, performance (often compared to a benchmark) and fees for any fund in the Key Investor Information Document (KIID), or factsheet. 'KIID' and 'factsheet' are two interchangeable names for the same document ('KIID' is a newer term, and technically the correct one these days, but lots of websites still use the term 'factsheet').

Then, there is that extra component for you to check. Not everyone does this last step, but in my humble opinion, they should:

4. Does the fund match your ethical criteria?

I'm not saying that everyone should invest ethically, though the fact you're reading this book suggests that you probably want to. I do however think that everyone should at least *know* how they're invested.

So how can you check?

Well, you can screen for different sectors – maybe you're not into alcohol and don't want your money to benefit that industry; perhaps you particularly want to invest in green energy solutions; or maybe you actually do want to invest in sectors and companies which you deem unethical in a bid to influence the company's future decisions – it's all possible. Welcome to Willy Wonka's Chocolate Factory – except, instead of chocolate, you have investments, and instead of an eccentric magician, you have a bespectacled bearded bloke in a tie (that's me) talking about investments as if they *were* chocolate.

~

As an aside, going back to pensions for a second – if you have a Personal Pension or a Workplace Pension which is no longer receiving contributions from your employer, you might have this level of fund choice in your pension too!

If you don't, you might be able to move your pension to one in which you could have this level of fund choice!

And for this reason, I think we can all agree, pensions are as exciting as investments, which, in turn, as we've already discussed, are as exciting as Willy Wonka's Chocolate Factory. *Charlie and the Chocolate Factory* was one of Gemma's favourite books as a child, and thus, pensions are exciting.

In a way, these are Gemma's own words.

I think that's a hands-down win.

What can you do?

Presumably you're starting from scratch, possibly with some money which is held in cash, or maybe you want to save a little bit each month. Because you're in the Willy Wonka's Chocolate Factory of Investment (a title which probably wouldn't have sold as well) you can start by sussing out what ethical investing means to you and then working backwards.

Whilst this sounds great, the reality is that you probably won't be able to accurately replicate your ideals (just as Willy Wonka hadn't quite managed to perfect his everlasting gobstoppers). Hopefully, though, this book will be able to help you find the form of investing which comes closest to what you're after, and that should help lead you to the right funds for you.

If what you're after doesn't exist yet, I would urge you not to get frustrated and go rogue. We're all idealists living in a realists' world...

To give you an example of what I mean, let's say you don't want to invest in tobacco. Well, that should be fairly simple. But let's say that not only do you not want to invest in tobacco, but you also don't want to invest in the supermarkets that sell tobacco — that's going to be harder. There's likely to be an element of humble pie in ethical investing for most people, but if enough people invest as best they can from what's available, this sends a message to the fund managers that the demand is there for more, and theoretically, when that happens, the options we have for our investments should grow over time. We will get that everlasting gobstopper, and it will last for ever.

Let's apply what we've learnt so far to my six-year-old...

One evening, Gemma and I put on a trashy reality TV programme (I won't tell you which one) and opened the laptop. We wanted to set up a regular investment for our six-year-old son. One day, when he's old enough, we'll give him the money, but that's going to be twelve years from now.

This morning, my son tried to convince me to buy him a Mini Moto (a small but very real motorbike) and if he carries on in that trajectory he'll be well into his forties before he sees the money.

Anyway, the first thing we needed to find was a suitable platform. Because of my job and how much I like to geek out about investments, I wanted to make sure that we picked a platform that could hold any fund available on the market. We only wanted to pick one fund for him, though, so this probably wasn't necessary. We could have found the right fund first, and then a platform which offered it after.

After that, we checked that the account could be viewed online (most platforms can be) and that the ongoing fee seemed fair (often between 0.30% and 0.50% of the value of the investment each year). Every provider will publish their fees, and there are comparison sites which can help you.

Once the account was open, we had to choose an investment. One day, when and if his investment grows to a decent amount, we'll move his money into a whole portfolio of funds, but there really isn't much point of investing £100

THE BASICS (REGULAR, RUN-OF-THE-MILL INVESTMENTS)

a month into lots of different funds, so we had to choose just one regular, run-of-the-mill investment.

We discussed the level of investment risk we'd be happy to take. Given that this money is going to be invested for a long time, and given that I understand the way the market works, we agreed we should take a relatively high level of investment risk with our son's money. I think he'd be happy with that too – I'd say he's pretty risky if the Mini Moto request is anything to go by.

As we were looking for just one fund, we searched for multi-asset funds to ensure that it would offer a certain level of diversification in and of itself. The website we were using (and there are lots, so I won't list them here)[1] offered three categories of multi-asset funds:

1. Mixed Investment 0–35% Shares
2. Mixed Investment 20–60% Shares
3. Mixed Investment 40–85% Shares

The different percentages refer to how much of the fund is invested in equities (shares in companies). The higher the percentage, the higher the risk level, so we decided to search 'Mixed Investment 40–85% Shares.' We were presented with over two hundred funds to choose from, which sounds like a lot, but before the filter was applied there were close to four thousand.

Most platforms, sadly, do not have a filter for any kind of ethical investment, let alone specific filters for different *sectors* or *types* of ethical investment, so now, theoretically,

---

1 Trustnet, Morningstar, Hargreaves Lansdown to name a few…

we'd have to go through the **KIID**s or factsheets for each of the over two hundred funds to look for, and read, the ethical statements (for the few funds which even have one). Well, that just wasn't feasible. For a start, the trashy reality TV programme we were watching only lasted an hour.

There are a few little tricks to finding the funds you're looking for though, which we'll go into later on in the book.

CHAPTER 4

Just a little bit of knowledge on the basics (banking)

I can't believe that Gemma hadn't considered the ethical effects of her pension – she is very irresponsible.

I'm also shocked that my six-year-old takes little to no interest in his investments – he takes so little interest, in fact, that he doesn't even know they exist.

At least no one in my family is getting their banking wrong. That would just be embarrassing… oh wait. That'll be me, then. And I'm a professional. Do we need to do this chapter?

OK, fine, so there are some very easy steps that you (I) can take to ensure that your (my) personal banking is as ethical as you (I) would like it to be. First, though, let's just get an idea of how it all works and why your (my) cash savings could be considered unethical.

In simple terms, you open a savings account with a bank and that bank agrees to pay you a certain amount of interest on the money, provided you leave that money in the account. From an investment risk perspective, it doesn't get much safer than this. Yes, your money might be worth less in the future because of inflation, but £100 with a 2.5% annual interest rate will be valued at £102.50 next year (ignoring compound interest). Great, that's a pack of football stickers.

But where does the interest actually come from?

The bank will pool your money together with other people's, and use it to make loans. Yes, some of these loans are to people, but more importantly, a very large chunk of this money is loaned to companies.

The bank charges these companies a higher interest rate than they're offering you. They buy your money for a low cost, and then sell it for more.

In return for your money, you're offered a safe place to hold the cash (normally covered up to a certain amount by the Government) and interest at the lowest rate in the chain.

Whether you'd consider a bank to be ethical or not ultimately comes down to two things:

1. **Their lending criteria:** Who and what are they making loans to, and which industries do these loans support. The banks want loans to yield the highest interest rates possible. This makes the bank more money and allows them to offer you, the consumer, higher interest rates, which in turn makes them more competitive. This then brings in new consumers who deposit more capital, which again, will be loaned out, and so the cycle continues. Have you ever considered which companies your bank might be lending your money to? Not many people have, which ultimately makes it easier for the banks to let profit drive their decisions over the ethical beliefs of their customers, i.e. you (and, yes, me).

2. **The bank as a company itself:** It might be that your bank has an ethical statement (which will likely cover the bank itself and the bank's lending criteria), though this isn't necessarily the case. If they do, it's a good indication that they are one of the good ones.

If they don't, the financial press will have published articles on your bank's ethical standing. These will be especially easy to find if it's not a good one.

What can you do?

Ethical banking is a young area in the finance world, so the banks which have the highest ethical lending criteria are normally advertising themselves as being ethical, which makes this whole process easier. They're also the ones who will be the most forthcoming with their lending criteria and ethical statements, because that'll be a selling point for them. So, what you can do really comes down to a minimal amount of research followed by an instruction to move your money to the new chosen bank.

Let's apply what we've learnt so far to me...

As I mentioned in the book's introduction, I opened my bank account when I was sixteen and then used it for twenty-two years without ever questioning it. At some point I've opened a savings account with the same bank, and that has gone up and down over time as I saved and withdrew money from it. With my son's future in mind (and, not to be too dramatic, but also with the *world's* future in mind), I looked at the ethical standing of my chosen bank. They're one of the big ones. I wasn't going to name them, but, well, go on then, you've pushed me. It's HSBC.

I requested their lending criteria, along with an ethical statement, but was told that there is no such publicly available document. I was offered the lending criteria for individuals (i.e. for me to personally take out a loan), but it wasn't relevant and showed a misunderstanding of my request.

Disheartened by the lack of interest my bank was showing, I Googled 'How ethical is HSBC', and found that they lend to companies linked to nuclear weapons, deforestation and the Myanmar military, amongst other questionable industries. The bank also apparently has the biggest gender pay gaps of all banks in the UK.[1]

I wasn't looking forward to telling Gemma that her banking was more ethical than mine (remember what I do for a living), so I Googled:

- 'How ethical is Barclays'
- 'How ethical is NatWest'
- 'How ethical is Lloyds'
- 'How ethical is Santander'

...and repeat for the other high street banks.

I found that most high street banks are lending other people's money to all kinds of industries which I would consider unethical. It was genuinely quite eye-opening.

Next, I searched for the most ethical banks in the UK and was presented with a short list – a list which annoyingly included Gemma's bank. Triodos Bank came out as number one on the list, and so I promptly Googled them. Lo and behold, I was presented with lending criteria and minimum standards for investments. These included criteria for human dignity, planet awareness and governance (essentially the

---

[1] Ethical Consumer, 'HSBC' (December 2022).
https://www.ethicalconsumer.org/company-profile/hsbc

three components of ESG – see Chapter 8). Presuming Triodos are living up to their own stated criteria, they're miles ahead of most of the high-street banks.

I don't want to have to fess up to Gemma on this one. Don't get me wrong – it's good that there's progress in the banking world, but she's going to mock me for not switching banks earlier, and for good reason. But I guess it comes down to what you're most against – deforestation and gender pay gaps, or your wife mocking you – and as I've said throughout this book, ethics can be a personal thing.

I know where I sit on this issue.

~

It shouldn't have taken me twenty-two years to get to this point. Ultimately, all I've done here is a few simple Internet searches, and in leaving it this long I've let HSBC use my (admittedly pitiful) money to dirty their hands for over two decades. When I spoke to a HSBC representative, they had no concept of what I was asking. I made a few calls of the same ilk over a few days, and no one could help. Of course, HSBC are a huge multinational corporation with all sorts of departments in different places, and we can't expect everyone in a support centre to be able to help with this, but it does go to show how little this area of finance is progressing.

Comparing banks and then speaking with HSBC highlighted one crucial thing for me – I'm not alone. Change comes from the bottom up. If consumers (that's us) aren't asking the right questions and applying pressure on the banks, they will follow the profit with no consideration for the planet for as long as possible. We need to make personal changes en masse, otherwise there will be no drive for commercial change.

There are non-profits raising awareness (as an example, Brandalism carried out a huge campaign against Barclays during Wimbledon 2024),[1] and things must be moving in the right direction for banks such as Triodos to even exist. Now we just need to take advantage of this new heightened awareness to keep up momentum, and for the big boys (and the, ahem, less well-paid girls) to sit up and listen.

---

[1] 'Brandalism Slams Wimbledon's Barclays Link with Slew of Billboard Hacks', *Marketing Beat* (July 2024).
https://www.marketing-beat.co.uk/2024/07/01/barclays-wimbledon-ads/

CHAPTER 5

What a conventional fund typically invests in

Most of us don't know what our money is invested in, and when you consider the sheer size of the UK pension market alone (according to the Office for National Statistics, it was around £6.1 trillion in March 2018)[1] this feels criminal.

The great pension swindle

As I've already mentioned, Gemma's invested in the Aviva Managed fund. Not to shame Gemma, but I can tell you that her pension is worth around £2,500. It's not going to see her through retirement. When we get a takeaway, it costs £25 for two pizzas (with garlic mayo, obviously), so Gemma's pension equates to around a hundred takeaways in retirement (or two hundred individual pizzas, with garlic mayo, obviously). This assumes that the value of Gemma's pension keeps up with inflation, the cost of pizza increases with inflation, and so does the cost of garlic mayo.

---

1 Office for National Statistics, *Pension Wealth in Great Britain: April 2016 to March 2018* (December 2019).
https://www.ons.gov.uk/peoplepopulationandcommunity/personalandhouseholdfinances/incomeandwealth/bulletins/pensionwealthingreatbritain/april2016tomarch2018

It's not going to pay many bills.

According to Aviva's own factsheet (or KIID), the total size of the Aviva Managed fund was £3,371,150,000 at the end of August 2023. I personally find that a hard number to read, so in words, it's three billion, three hundred and seventy-one million, one hundred and fifty thousand pounds – or if you prefer, 134,846,000 takeaways (269,692,000 individual pizzas, with garlic mayo, obviously).

£2,500 is more than Gemma's pension was worth when she started it. Unsurprisingly, it wasn't worth anything when she first received the welcome letter through the post. This letter informed Gemma of the default fund, the Aviva Managed fund we've been talking about, and gave her a list of the thirty alternative funds she could invest in. If Gemma did nothing (which, remember, she did) her pension would be invested in the default fund.

When Gemma received this letter, she'd just started a new job and was in the process of settling in – new systems, new processes, new colleagues and a new coffee machine to understand. How she invested her seemingly completely empty pension was very low down on her priority list. The letter went on the kitchen side for a month or so, and then in a cupboard. No one touches that cupboard now – it's full of historical paperwork and we're worried that any kind of movement could force it to collapse.

As it happens, Gemma didn't stay at that company very long (she never could quite work out that coffee machine), but had she done so, her pension would have continued to grow from contributions, and eventually she'd be investing a reasonable portion of her overall income in a fund that she hadn't researched, and in company shares that she hadn't chosen.

WHAT A CONVENTIONAL FUND TYPICALLY INVESTS IN

The capital of most default pension funds is accumulated this way. They are huge collective investments that provide money to various companies, allowing them to grow. The people funding these collective investments are people like you and I, but the investments are normally chosen by the fund manager.

Contrary to what I said in my wedding vows, Gemma is not unique. Most people don't know which fund their pension is invested in, and many don't know who holds their pension or how to access information about it. Given the sheer size of the collective pot, and the relatively few companies benefiting from it, I think at the very least we need to know how our retirement money is being invested.

In Chapter 2 I listed the top ten companies and holdings that the Aviva Managed fund invests in (see p. 41). Using the collective value of the fund (£3,371,150,000), this table shows how much is being allocated to the top ten:

Holding	Percentage of fund	Value of investment	Or...*
US Treasury 1.123% Index-Linked 01/33	3.8%	£128,103,700	£128.1 million
Microsoft Corporation	1.9%	£64,051,850	£64.1 million
SPDR ETF Bloomberg Emerging Markets Local Bonds UCITS	1.5%	£50,567,250	£50.6 million
Apple	1.4%	£47,196,100	£47.2 million
UK Treasury Bill 0% 11/12/2023	1.2%	£40,453,800	£40.5 million
AstraZeneca	0.9%	£30,340,350	£30.3 million
Alphabet Incorporated	0.9%	£30,340,350	£30.3 million
Shell	0.8%	£26,969,200	£27.0 million
Amazon.com	0.7%	£23,598,050	£23.6 million
Nestlé S.A	0.7%	£23,598,050	£23.6 million
Unaccounted for	**86.2%**	**£2,905,931,300**	**£2 billion, 905.9 million**

*Rounded to the nearest £100,000.

Using Nestlé as an example, I'm not for a second suggesting that Gemma is investing £23.6 million of her hard-earned pension with Nestlé, because, like I say, Gemma only has £2,500 in her pension. She is investing £17.50 of her pension in Nestlé, though, and hundreds of thousands of other people are investing 0.7% of their pensions in Nestlé too.

And again, I'm not judging; as we've already discovered, I love a KitKat, so why should I hold Gemma's pension up to standards above my own? I've definitely spent more than £17.50 on KitKats in my life. The point I'm making isn't to boycott KitKats (I tried that at university once and it's harder than it sounds), it's that Gemma, and most other people invested in the Aviva Managed fund, don't *know* that they're investing in KitKats, or more precisely, Nestlé.

And yet, that information is freely available – it's written in the KIID/factsheet. When I told Gemma that she had around £17.50 of her pension invested in Nestlé, she told me that she wanted to change her investment. She remembers the baby-milk scandal of the seventies (despite her not being alive then), and, if possible, she doesn't want to support the company in any way. It probably helps that she's lactose intolerant. I'd like to take such a stand, but as I believe I've already mentioned, I just love a KitKat.

With Gemma's general outrage at Nestlé in mind, let's look at the last row of the table, which I've called 'unaccounted for'. Fund managers only list their top ten holdings, and in this case, that accounts for 13.8% of the fund, leaving a whopping 86.2% of the fund unaccounted for.

This equates to roughly £2,905,931,300. Again, I find that a hard number to read, so in words, it's two billion, nine hundred and five million, nine hundred and thirty-one

WHAT A CONVENTIONAL FUND TYPICALLY INVESTS IN

thousand, three hundred pounds. This is the collective money of regular people like you and I, invested into undisclosed companies. Or, if you're just here for the pizza chat, it's 116,237,252 takeaways (or 232,474,504 individual pizzas, with garlic mayo, obviously). In fact, of the whole Aviva Managed fund, we've only accounted for 37,217,496 individual pizzas with garlic mayo so far.

So, if Gemma wasn't happy about her investment with Nestlé, I'm sure you can guess how she felt about the portion of her pension invested in undisclosed companies.

Unfortunately, short of investing in direct shares (which, as we discussed earlier, is close to impossible to do whilst managing risk in a pension), there isn't much she can do about this particular smokescreen, and that's because if fund managers listed every holding in a fund, other fund managers would be able to replicate the fund, and the fund manager in question would lose any kind of competitive advantage. The full list of holdings is their intellectual property, so we can't expect them to release this information. For those people looking to invest ethically, though, especially for people with strong opinions on certain companies, like Gemma, this can be frustrating.

Whilst we can't look at the full list of specific *holdings* and *companies* a fund invests in, with the right software we can look at which *industries* and *sectors* the fund invests in. There are publicly available web pages which allow you to do this, which we'll look at in Chapter 13. Full disclosure, though: here we're going to be using a subscription-based industry software called 'Capita Synaptic'. Capita Synaptic works in the same way as the publicly available websites, but also has a few extra flourishes which have helped with the research of this book. You don't need these extra flourishes, though, so to all intents and purposes it's the same.

The system allows us to filter different sectors either in, or out, of a search for investments. For example, I can filter to show only investment funds which aim to have a positive focus on climate-change management, or I can filter to show only investment funds which aim to avoid companies involved in the production and/or distribution of alcohol. It does get a little complicated here.

First, the filter can only take the fund manager's word for it.

Second, a fund may well have a policy of aiming to avoid companies involved in the production and distribution of alcohol, but the specifics can be hazy. We touched on this earlier in the book, but there are funds which make this claim but then invest a percentage of the capital in supermarkets. Of course, alcohol is sold in supermarkets, but that isn't the supermarket's sole purpose. This is what I mean by 'hazy' – there is an element of discretion on the fund manager's behalf. It would be fair to say, though, that a fund aiming not to invest in the production and distribution of alcohol would not invest in Smirnoff or Bargain Booze.

Given how opaque the workings of any fund are, there must be an element of trust, along with an acceptance that it's not going to be perfect.

We have to pay attention to that word 'aim' when we look at what the fund managers are doing. They *aim* to avoid companies involved in the production and/or distribution of alcohol, but they can't guarantee it. This sounds like a method of avoiding accountability, and maybe it is to a certain degree, but it's also necessary.

WHAT A CONVENTIONAL FUND TYPICALLY INVESTS IN

Consider: several ethical funds will hold Microsoft as a top ten holding. Microsoft is huge, so it could probably be argued that one of the many arms of Microsoft is directly or indirectly distributing or at least marketing alcohol. Outlook is a Microsoft product, and Outlook adverts are selected by an algorithm, so there is every chance that an advert for an alcoholic product could sneak its way in there. This is just a basic example, but there are many, so it's not reasonable to expect a guarantee from a fund manager. Different people have different standards, and companies are living, ever-changing entities.

It is reasonable to expect fund managers to *aim* to achieve whatever it is they're claiming to do, though.

Let's look at the Aviva Managed fund. The first relevant filter available on Capita Synaptic is simply, 'Ethical Fund'. I can tell you that, by using this basic filter, the Aviva Managed fund instantly disappears.

What does that mean? It means that the Aviva Managed fund doesn't aim to be an ethical fund – which is fine, it never said it did.

I told Gemma this and she asked me what the fund disappearing under this very basic filter specifically means for *her* money.

Well, I told her with the smug face of someone who already had a list of bullet points to hand, it means that the fund doesn't aim to invest in companies which:

- Support the basic necessities (essentially, supporting the absolute minimum for physical wellbeing for people below the poverty line)
- Support community involvement

- Support clean energy or renewable energy
- Support climate-change management
- Support environmental management
- Support equal opportunities
- Support healthcare, safety and wellbeing
- Support positive labour relations
- Support positive sustainability strategies
- Support sustainable development
- Support training and education
- Avoid alcohol production
- Avoid animal intensive farming (retail or wholesale)
- Avoid animal testing (cosmetics or pharmaceuticals)
- Avoid banks and financial institutions
- Avoid coal, oil or gas extraction
- Avoid environmental abuse
- Avoid gambling
- Avoid human-rights abuse
- Avoid military
- Avoid nuclear energy
- Avoid pornography
- Avoid tobacco

'It also means,' I told Gemma, looking up from my list, 'that the Aviva Managed fund doesn't aim to better the business practices of the companies it invests in. It could do this through shareholder voting, but it doesn't, and it isn't supporting the development of other ethical investments.'

Gemma was cross – partly with me for reading the list out loud rather than just giving it to her, but mostly with the conduct of the fund.

WHAT A CONVENTIONAL FUND TYPICALLY INVESTS IN

But why would the fund aim to do these things? It doesn't claim to be an ethical fund. And because it doesn't claim to be an ethical fund, it also doesn't measure the positive impact of its investment strategy, though presumably if it did, it wouldn't take long.

The list above doesn't mean that the fund *does* invest in (for example) pornography and companies with poor human-rights records. It just means that it can, and that we simply cannot know if it does, because the full list of holdings is never published. Honestly, though, with the low level of accountability that comes from not sharing the full list of holdings, I'd be surprised if it didn't.

As I've said before, I'm not out to get the Aviva Managed fund (for starters, with £3,371,150,000 under its belt, I doubt I'd win any court cases). The Aviva Managed fund really is your everyday, run-of-the-mill, conventional/traditional investment/pension fund. I'm just using Gemma's pension as a way of emphasising how little people know about what their pensions are invested in.

To give you an idea of just how average the Aviva Managed fund is, I've used Capita Synaptic to filter for all the funds which could reasonably be used as a default fund in a UK Defined Contribution pension. There are 2,852 funds in this search. This isn't to say that they're all being used as default funds, just that they could be, based on the way they invest.

Next, I added the filter 'Ethical Fund', and the list is reduced to just 176 funds. This places the Aviva Managed fund with the 93.8% of these funds which do not aim to invest in an ethical manner.

Using some of the examples from the earlier list, that means that all these funds could be investing in alcohol, animal intensive farming, animal testing, banks and financial institutions, coal, oil or gas extraction, environmental abuse, gambling, human-rights abuse, military, nuclear energy, pornography or tobacco. Likewise, the fund managers have no duty to consider whether the companies they invest in support community, clean energy, climate change and environmental management, equal opportunities, safety or wellbeing, positive labour relations, sustainability strategies/ development or education.

I'm not being alarmist here. There's a reason why these filters are used for ethical investors. It's because traditional funds *are* investing in these sectors.

For the sake of pizza maths, let's assume that each of these funds holds the same amount of capital as the Aviva Managed fund. They won't − some will hold more, some will hold less; but if they did, this would equate to £9,021,197,400,000 (nine trillion, twenty-one billion, one hundred and ninety-seven million, four hundred thousand pounds). Assuming each of these funds have top ten holdings equating to around 13.8% of the overall fund, that's £7,776,272,158,800 (seven trillion, seven hundred and seventy-six billion, two hundred and seventy-two million, one hundred and fifty-eight thousand, eight hundred pounds) of unaccounted-for capital being invested in companies and holdings which are undisclosed, by fund managers with no (or limited) ethical restrictions or aims.

Now to the good stuff... It equates to 324,011,339,950 pizza takeaways for me and Gemma, which is 648,022,679,900 individual pizzas (with garlic mayo, obviously).

Man, I really want a pizza now.

WHAT A CONVENTIONAL FUND TYPICALLY INVESTS IN

~

I've found that most people find it hard to believe that their traditionally invested pensions are benefiting gambling companies or the sex trade. Some people specifically want to ensure that they are actively investing in renewable energy, and for others it's the avoidance of human-rights abuse which is most important. Sometimes I meet people who want to filter for almost the entire list but are happy to invest a portion of their pension into military and armaments. Everyone is different, but for each filter adopted, the choice of funds reduces.

As I said before, you can't filter specific companies, so Gemma may still find herself invested in Nestlé through some quirk, but she can filter to exclude companies with a low human-rights data scoring (for example), which might limit investment in Nestlé, if not fully exclude it.

Interestingly, you can't filter to show funds which support pizza consumption, which is strange, considering how relevant it is.

A note on Nest

We all like to hate on the Government, right? This bit will be fun…

In Chapter 2 we talked about Workplace Pensions, and how, in 2012, employers became required by law to enrol their employees into a Workplace Pension. All employees earning over £10,000, aged over twenty-two and below State Pension age were, and continue to be, eligible. The auto-enrolment rules meant that all employers had a duty to provide a Workplace Pension for their workers. They had to select a pension and then make contributions into each member's policy (unless that member had opted out).

For some businesses this was an absolute pain, and the Government knew it. Most small business owners – those without a HR department – are busy, and this was just one extra job.

'No worries,' said the Government, 'we've created this problem, and so we'll fix it.'

Nest was set up to be an easy one-stop shop for a Workplace Pension. Nest stands for National Employment Savings Trust, and was created by the Government for employers to fulfil their obligations to provide a Workplace Pension. Any employer trying to tick the legal box of providing a pension to employees could use Nest and know, without any shadow of doubt, that they'd done what they had to do to meet the requirements.

I believe that auto-enrolment is fundamentally a good thing. The country is full of people without a pension, and life is too expensive and busy for a huge portion of the population to even think about setting one up. Retirement does come eventually, for most people at least, and the new rules make having a pension the starting point rather than an afterthought, BUT…

…Here are some facts about Nest:

1. According to the Nest website, the scheme now has 11 million members and counting. It is one of the world's fastest-growing pension schemes by member numbers,[1] meaning businesses (and therefore people) are signing up to the scheme all the time. This, despite countless other providers offering lower-cost Workplace Pensions with greater investment choice.

---

[1] Nest Insight, 'About Nest Insight' (August 2024). https://www.nestinsight.org.uk/about-nest-insight

WHAT A CONVENTIONAL FUND TYPICALLY INVESTS IN

2. Over 99% of Nest members are invested in Nest Retirement Date Funds.[1] These are funds which are set up to lower the risk of your pension the closer you come to retirement (meaning the money is less likely to drop in value the closer you come to using it). This is the default option, so it's no wonder over 99% of Nest members are invested this way – that high percentage really emphasises the lack of engagement people have with their pension investments.

3. Credit where credit's due: Under the 'How does it work' section on the Nest website, specifically referring to the Nest Retirement Date Funds (Nest's default funds), it does state: *'We were one of the first pension providers to commit to net zero carbon emissions. We also promote workers' rights, knowing that members like you make up a majority of the UK's workforce. Actions like this form part of a strategy carefully crafted with you and your future in mind, as we believe it's likely to make more money for you over time.'* Hey, that's positive, right?

4. Well, yes, it's an excellent message, but Nest does offer another five funds to choose from. While five is limited, one of the other funds is called the Nest Ethical Fund, which aims to avoid companies which:

    a. Don't follow human-rights conventions or UK and international labour standards;
    b. Own geological reserves of oil, gas or coal;
    c. Use or trade threatened species;
    d. Don't actively try to minimise pollution;

---

[1] Nest, 'Nest Retirement Date Fund' (August 2024). https://www.nestpensions.org.uk/schemeweb/nest/investing-your-pension/fund-choices/retirement-date-fund.html

e. Engage in controversial mining and quarrying practices such as fracking;
   f. Don't follow a clear code of ethics;
   g. Are involved in bribery or corruption;
   h. Make their money from creating or selling weapons, weapons systems or weapons components;
   i. Test cosmetics on animals or are involved in the trade of animal fur;
   j. Are in tobacco, alcohol, pornography or gambling industries.

And actively invests in companies which:
   a. Take steps to reduce their carbon-intensive footprint;
   b. Are developing solutions such as renewable energy infrastructure and low-carbon technologies;
   c. Have strong environmental policies, reporting and management;
   d. Look after biodiversity and the environment;
   e. Take good care of the world's water supply;
   f. Have a clear code of ethics;
   g. Follow principles laid down by the UN Global Compact;
   h. Have a diverse board with separation between the roles of chief executive and chairperson;
   i. Meet animal welfare codes of practice relevant to their industry.

Whilst the Nest Retirement Date Funds (the default funds) do commit to net zero carbon emissions, and do claim to promote workers' rights, they don't make the same commitments that the Nest Ethical Fund does. The Nest Retirement Date funds don't specifically make the same promises, and certainly there is nothing measurable. Notice, for example, that the Nest Ethical fund avoids companies that don't follow human-rights conventions. No such promise is made for the Nest Retirement Date funds, despite claiming to promote workers' rights. Similarly, the Nest Ethical fund avoids companies that engage in fracking, or own geological reserves of oil, gas or coal. Whilst the Nest Retirement Date funds do commit to net zero carbon emissions, they don't state that they avoid these companies in the same way the Nest Ethical fund does. The Nest Retirement Date funds do state that they're in the process of excluding the fossil-fuel companies which won't help to achieve the net zero target, but it's a process, and one without any clear specifics or time frames. In a nutshell, the Nest Ethical fund makes commitments which are more easily measured and offer better clarity on the inner workings of the fund. However, going back to that original figure, the Nest Retirement Date funds account for over 99% of the Nest pot.

I've decided to write about Nest in this chapter because it's such a huge pension scheme, and relevant to so many people – 11 million members equates to over 16% of the UK's population, and let's not forget that a decent chunk of the UK's population is taken up by children and the elderly. According to the Office for National Statistics, from October to December 2024, UK employment rate was 74.9%,[1] which means that roughly 21% of the working population have a Nest pension.

---

[1] Office for National Statistics, *Employment in the UK: February 2025* (February 2025).
https://www.ons.gov.uk/employmentandlabourmarket/peopleinwork/employmentandemployeetypes/bulletins/employmentintheuk/latest#Employment

If you work and you're reading this book, there is a roughly one in five chance that this is directly relevant to you. If it is, you should know that the Nest Ethical fund can also decrease the level of risk it takes as you near your retirement, similar to the Nest Retirement Date funds, if that's what you're after. They are both considered to be in the same risk level in the growth phase (long before retirement), and they have provided very similar returns. According to the Nest website in December 2024, the Nest Retirement Date funds in growth phase have performed better than the Nest Ethical fund by 1.1% annualised over the past five years, and since the launch of the funds, the Nest Ethical fund has performed better than the Nest Retirement Date funds in the growth stage by 0.6% annualised.[1]

I should remind you here that pensions tend to be invested for multiple decades.

And yet, over 99% of members (and 99% of 11 million people is 10.89 million) are invested in the Nest Retirement Date funds. In Nest's *Corporation Annual Report and Accounts 2022/23* it states that the scheme holds just under £30 billion of assets.[2] This is the collective savings of regular people like you and I, most of whom are not paying attention to how their money is invested. That number is around nine times

---

[1] Nest, 'Compare Nest pension fund performance' (December 2024). https://www.nestpensions.org.uk/schemeweb/nest/investing-your-pension/fund-choices/compare-fund-performance.html

[2] Nest, *Nest, the National Employment Savings Trust: Corporation Annual Report and Accounts 2022/23* (2023). https://assets.publishing.service.gov.uk/media/652fef0cd0666200131b7cbd/nest-annual-report-and-accounts-2022-to-2023.pdf

more than those huge numbers we were talking about when we were looking at the Aviva Managed fund.

It's a big deal, and I don't even want to think about how many pizzas it would buy (1.2 billion pizza takeaways, or 2.4 billion individual pizzas, with garlic mayo, obviously).

It's strange, when you think about it, that Nest aren't making the Nest Ethical fund the default fund. Imagine the positive message that would send to the companies Nest funds invest in.

If you do have a Nest pension, I'm not saying that it's bad, and I'm not here to tell you how to invest either. I'm just here to tell you to check that your pension is invested how *you* want it to be invested, not how the scheme (read: Government) does. You'll find more information on these funds (and the other 4) on the Nest website.[1]

---

1 See https://www.nestpensions.org.uk/schemeweb/nest.html.

CHAPTER 6

The limited world of an ethical six-year-old (investments outside your pension)

When Gemma and I started saving money for our six-year-old, we had a long discussion around what we did and didn't want his money to be invested in. My big worry was that he'd reach eighteen and refuse to spend it because it had profited from something he didn't believe in, such as deforestation (although he still brings sticks back home, so maybe he's cool with it).

I don't think this is a worry most people have. There aren't many people paying attention to the inner workings of their kid's investments – partly because they don't know how to, and partly because they just don't believe that traditional investments *would* be profiting from deforestation (or something equally as terrible).

The other reason I don't think people have my specific worry is because, ultimately, most eighteen-year-olds probably wouldn't turn down the money regardless.

In an ideal world, though, Gemma and I would like our six-year-old's investments to filter out all the sectors which are considered unethical. Equally, we'd like his money to benefit the companies that are actively doing good in the world. But sadly, the world of ethical investment funds just doesn't work like that.

~

To give you an idea of what we (and possibly you) are working with, I've carried out a basic filtering task to show just how young the world of ethical investment is. For the sake of housekeeping, I should say that I'm only looking at open-ended investment funds here, which just means that the shares/units in the fund can be bought and sold, and the value of each share/unit reflects the fund's assets. More to the point, it means that I'm not looking at every possible investment fund you could choose, but the ratios do reflect the market now.

Let's say we had no interest in ethically screening our son's investments. We would have a choice of 3,157 open-ended investment funds to choose from. That's a huge amount of choice, which sparks competition amongst the fund managers.

But we *do* want to ethically screen our son's investments, so the first thing we do is remove any fund without any ethical criteria. This leaves us with 436 funds.

This means, as it stands now, just under 14% of the UK open-ended investment fund market has an ethical criterion.

This is a huge improvement from only ten years ago, when the number was less than half that, but it still isn't the fine selection you might think. A fund which actively avoids investing in alcohol, for example, may well be invested in companies with bad human-rights records. To narrow your choices down, you have to decide what matters most to you.

Using the list of different screening criteria in Chapter 5, I've filtered the 436 funds to show how, by filtering just one sector, your choices become even more limited:

Sector	Number of funds
Supports:	
Basic necessities	38
Community involvement	28
Clean or renewable energy	50
Climate-change management	50
Environmental management	49
Equal opportunities	45
Healthcare, safety and wellbeing	50
Positive labour relations	49
Positive sustainability strategies	50
Sustainable development	46
Training and education	42
Avoids:	
Alcohol production	56
Animal intensive farming	30
Animal testing (cosmetics)	54
Animal testing (pharmaceuticals)	27
Banks and financial institutions	5
Coal, oil or gas extraction	51
Environmental abuse	48
Gambling	57
Human-rights abuse	52
Military	61
Nuclear energy	50
Pornography	56
Tobacco	64
Other	
Shareholder advocacy and engagement	55

It doesn't leave much room for virtue. Let's say that our six-year-old feels quite strongly about supporting equal opportunities, and that he would hate for his money to benefit the animal intensive farming industry (or 'lots of moo-cow', as he might once have put it). Just by doubling his criteria, he's reduced his options from forty-five funds which support equal opportunities, and thirty funds which avoid animal intensive farming, to just eighteen funds which do both.

Don't get me wrong, there are lots of crossovers, but it is easy to quickly limit your options. The more stringent your criteria, the more limited your options become. If you filter for all the criteria, you're left with nothing, which is a shame, because that would be an easy win.

After a lot of playing around, Gemma and I decided to invest our son's savings in funds that avoid gambling, tobacco, pornography and armaments. These are generally known as the 'sin sectors' in the industry, and because of this well-known phrase, we were left with fifty-six funds to choose from.

In my experience, by filtering these sectors out, you tend to get a leaning towards some of the other sectors on the criteria list, but unless a fund specifies it, this is by no means a guarantee. It's a case of doing what you can and finding what is right for you (or in our case, our child).

None of this has really helped me with my worry. In twelve years, my then eighteen-year-old son still might refuse to spend the money. He could still reprimand me and Gemma for not investing in line with his own beliefs. After all, we still haven't filtered his investments for deforestation. But then, it was never an explicit option, and at least we've tried. You can't beat yourself up over these things.

It isn't like he's the most ethical person anyway. There was an altercation at school the other day, and I asked him what he should do if someone else is in the wrong. I expected him to say tell a teacher, but instead he told me he would 'poo on them'.

You just can't filter for that kind of thing.

CHAPTER 7

Supports, avoids, screening terms and 'other'

In the last chapter we started to 'screen', which is mostly relevant to Personal Pensions and investments outside of a pension. Workplace Pensions tend to only offer one or a select few ethical fund choices, though, and for that reason, my six-year-old has more flexibility with his money than Gemma.

Assuming Gemma doesn't transfer her Aviva pension to a different provider, she has thirty funds to choose from, so her screening will go something like this:

'Does the fund have the word 'ethical', 'sustainable', 'stewardship' or 'responsible' in its name?
No – Don't buy
Yes – Maybe buy

And given that there are thirty funds in total, she'll probably find one or two which fit the very loose and non-specific bill. That doesn't mean those funds will or won't be brilliant, it just means her research can be done, and she can sit back with a cuppa.

But the kiddo… he'll need to decide what kind of screening he wants before he can even start to get into the nitty-gritty of specific sectors. Hang on – I'll read that last sentence back to him and let you know what he says…

He says he wants 'a football screen – a Harry Kane one'.

I guess I'd better explain what the different screening processes are, along with a few other ways to invest ethically. (I'll read them to him when I'm done and let you know what he says.)

Positive screening

In the last chapter I referred to this type of screening as 'supports'. It's the equivalent of an investor saying: 'OK, so, I *do* want to invest in companies which (for example) provide green energy and have good human-rights records.' In Chapter 6 there is a list of eleven sectors which you can positively screen for. There are others, but the more niche you become, the more limited your options.

Screening for 'football' – or, more specifically, 'Harry Kane' – would be considered positive screening, but it would be a very high-risk strategy and a complicated process for your everyday investor. Also, whilst I have nothing against Harry Kane or any other footballer, I'm not sure investing in FIFA would be considered ethical.

Negative screening

If positive screening is actively trying to invest in certain sectors, it won't surprise you that negative screening is the opposite. It's the equivalent of an investor saying: 'OK, so, I *don't* want to invest in companies which (for example) produce tobacco or manufacture weapons.' In Chapter 6 there is a list of eleven common sectors which can be negatively screened.

This is also called divesting. There is a huge amount of discussion around whether divesting works as a method of future change. The argument goes, if you divest from BP (for example), other investors will continue to place their money there. Theoretically, BP doesn't really lose out, it just has less ethically minded shareholders, and of course it's the shareholders that drive a company. If literally everyone divested, BP would collapse, but that just isn't going to happen.

You might remember from this book's introduction that Gemma and I decided we didn't want our six-year-old invested in gambling, tobacco, armaments or pornography and the sex industry. This is negative screening, so here seems as good a place as any to explain our reasons for choosing this approach.

Unlike with fossil fuels, it doesn't seem likely that tobacco companies will change their practices. They sell tobacco and will continue to sell tobacco, and as far as I can see, tobacco only causes harm to people. Likewise, I just don't see my six-year-old's money contributing much towards an ethical future in the worlds of gambling and pornography. Finally, whilst armaments are necessary for national security, I refuse to buy my six-year-old a plastic gun, so it just makes sense to me that I shouldn't put what small amount of money he has into real guns. This last choice is likely to be the most controversial to some people, but remember, ethics is a personal thing.

As I've said before, we haven't negatively screened our son's money for fossil-fuel companies. I've given a hint as to why above, but I'll explain more in the next couple of sections...

Best in class

Although my son's investments aren't negatively screened for fossil fuels, just by negatively screening for the other four sectors listed in the previous section, he'll be holding what are considered to be ethical funds. It is therefore likely that the shares in fossil-fuel companies his funds are holding will be considered 'best in class'. Likely, but not guaranteed.

'Best in class' means that the fund manager will invest in the company which has either the best practices, the greatest focus on a positive transition to alternative fuels, or some other measure that can be used to compare the different fossil-fuel companies.

There is no hard-and-fast rule here, and there isn't normally anything written in the fund's ethical statement, so it's down to the fund manager's discretion, but there is some comfort in the knowledge that effort is being made somewhere, right?

Right?

RIGHT?!

It helps me sleep at night, anyway.

Stewardship

Stewardship funds set out to change the practices of certain companies using shareholder rights, actively engaging with the companies in which they're invested. They often have 'stewardship' in the fund name so they're quite easy to find.

To simplify things, there are two ways a stewardship fund can effect change. The first is to vote at Annual General

Meetings (AGMs) and the second is to start a vote. The stewardship process goes something like this:

1. The fund might write an engagement letter to the company in question. For example, the fund may write a letter requesting a company increase their carbon emission reduction target and bring forward the target date. If the company agrees at this stage, the request goes to a negotiation table to agree a specific outcome. If the company does not agree, we move to step two.
2. Step two is a vote to influence the outcome of step one. For example, this could be something along the lines of, 'The current CEO of Sustainability isn't taking the appropriate steps, and therefore we vote to remove them from their post.' I've been told on good authority that this step is often successful, and then you go to the negotiation table in step one, but if it isn't successful, we move on to step three.
3. An Annual General Meeting (AGM) will have a list of votes which the company themselves put on the agenda, and then a list of votes which the shareholders have put on the agenda. This is called 'shareholder resolution'. Continuing with our previous example, this could be a vote on the original request in the engagement letter as to whether the company should increase its carbon emission reduction target and bring forward the target date, or whether no change is needed. I've been told that roughly a 40% vote in favour of the request will trigger the company to illustrate what they have done, and what they will do, to resolve the request, and roughly a 70% vote in

favour means the company must follow through and deliver on the outcome of the vote.

If the vote is unsuccessful, the fund can ultimately divest itself of the company's shares, though we have already seen the potential flaws in this method. Other, less ethically minded investors come along and make it easier for the company to make what we might consider to be the wrong decisions in future AGMs. However, it's this threat of divestment that is held over the company throughout the process, from stage one to stage three.

~

Hopefully this chapter has helped to explain some of the basic ways in which you can invest ethically. Some funds try to do a catch-all, so, for example, if you were to choose to *negatively* screen your investments, you'd probably find an element of *positive* screening in your results. You might also find that Stewardship fund managers are already negatively and/or positively screening their investments to a certain degree. Within all these funds, Best in Class tends to be common practice. Ultimately, fund managers want to attract as many investors as possible, so the more their funds show up under different screening processes, the better.

For fullness, it's probably worth mentioning the effect screening can have on the volatility of your investments. Remember, funds invest in hundreds, if not thousands of companies, which ensures that the overall fund has an increased level of stability. By taking out a whole sector, you reduce the number of types of companies that can be invested in, which can increase the volatility of the fund (the amount it goes up or down with the market). This is particularly the case with fossil-fuel companies, which often take up a fair portion of a traditional fund's investment. This is discussed in much more detail in Chapter 10, under 'Myth three' (see p. 116).

At the beginning of this chapter I said I'd read out these options to my son to see what he'd like to do. Well, I've done that, and he says, 'Yeah, the yes one, for Harry Kane.'

It's not a useful answer, but you know what? It does show some sort of understanding – not only of ethical screening, but also for the meaning of the word positive, so I'm going to email his teacher asking if he can skip his English homework this week. Well done, kiddo.

I'm still going to negatively screen his investments, though.

CHAPTER 8

A brief foray into the sexy world of terminology

There are other terms which you might come across when putting this into practice. They're all sexier ways of saying 'ethical'. You can feel awkward when these terms show up on the screen in front of your parents, or you can read this chapter to learn about these various 'kinks', and gain confidence.

Let's see if that analogy gets past my editor...

Anyway, the industry is full of jargon (that's the industry of ethical finance, not the sex industry, although I'll bet that is too), so I'll quickly go through some of the most common terms that you're likely to come across here:

ESG

This stands for 'Environmental, Social and Governance'. ESG funds consider these three areas, alongside more traditional investment considerations such as growth. Breaking down the three areas in turn, you have:

- 'Environmental', which might include considerations of carbon emissions and/or deforestation;
- 'Social', which might include data security and human-rights considerations;

- 'Governance', which focuses more on things like executive pay, for example, or the diversity of board members.

ESG fund managers analyse these three areas to understand the risks that companies run by not embracing ESG considerations, alongside the gains companies might make by embracing ESG opportunities. It's very data driven and forward facing, whilst still using traditional investment methodology.

SRI

This stands for 'Socially Responsible Investment', and tends to go a little further than ESG funds. SRI funds might add or eliminate certain sectors from investment based on a certain ethical criterion. If you're thinking, *That sounds familiar*, it's because we've been talking about it quite a lot in the last chapter. Lots of SRI funds will be ESG funds. They're different, but they often overlap.

Impact investing

This refers to investment which actively attempts to change company practices for social good. The Stewardship method, discussed in the last chapter, is an example of impact investing.

Light and dark green

If a fund is advertising a shade of green, it is just referring to the level of sustainability/ESG focus the fund has. Light green refers to funds which promote environmental or social characteristics, and dark green refers to funds which have sustainability as the sole objective. To refer back to an earlier analogy which may or may not be in this book by the time it's published, dark-green funds are the real hardcore stuff. You wouldn't want your mother to see those ones…

~

If you're investing ethically, you'll most likely be using one of, or a combination of, ESG, SRI or impact funds. The differences are important, but the multitude of different terms crowding the Internet makes the basic process of ethical investing feel impossible to your casual, socially conscious, investor. Take note of the differences, but don't let it bog you down so much that you don't take any action, and after exploring each term, if you find that missionary is your thing, that's cool.

CHAPTER 9

What an ethical fund typically invests in

It feels good to know that you're investing ethically. It gives you a warm feeling –

maybe even, dare I say it, a smug feeling? I think it's OK to acknowledge that.

I don't know how many people down the pub are telling their mates that they have an ethical pension, but I bet the people with an ethical pension are bringing it up more than the ones with a regular pension. In my own personal experience, career aside, I've had friends tell me they've invested their pension ethically without me asking.

I've never had anyone go on to explain what it means, though.

No one has said to me: 'Yeah, so, I've invested in this ethical fund, and what that means is…' and then gone on to list specific companies the fund supports. This chapter aims to help you tell your mates in the pub how you've invested your pension (although if you're negatively screening for alcohol, I'd give that part a miss)…

And whatever you do, don't bang on about your bamboo toothbrush.

~

The title of this chapter is misleading for two reasons:

1. There are lots of different ethical funds, and different types of ethical fund (and after those last two chapters, don't we just know it), so there is no real 'typical';
2. And just like with conventional funds, most of the data isn't disclosed. Again, intellectual property, blah blah blah. So again, there's only so far which we can delve, but delve we will…

You may remember in Chapters 2 and 5 we took a deep dive into the Aviva Managed fund on behalf of Gemma (I mean, come on Gemma, do your own research). You may also remember that she wasn't happy with many of the top ten underlying holdings of the Aviva Managed fund.

Gemma decided to switch her pension investment into Aviva's equivalent ethical fund – the Aviva Stewardship Managed fund.

Remember, Gemma has £2,500 in her pension, so this move isn't going to change the world, but as I've said before, if enough people were to make a similar switch, it would send a message – to fund managers, providers and the companies seeking investment. Consider every pound to be a tiny message in a fund-shaped bottle.

And it doesn't take as much as you'd think to effect change. If this book sells only half the amount my previous two fiction books did, and everyone who bought it made an ethical switch in their pension to the same value of Gemma's, that would be around 6,250,000 tiny messages in fund-shaped bottles.

You're welcome to do the maths, but remember I've broken it down into individual pounds, so this isn't a humble brag, believe me.

WHAT AN ETHICAL FUND TYPICALLY INVESTS IN

Let's do some basic comparison first. Let's look at the total value of the Aviva Managed fund (the default fund for many Workplace Pension plans) against the total value of the Aviva Stewardship Managed fund:

	Aviva Managed	**Aviva Stewardship Managed**
Numbers	£3,371,150,000	£845,750,000
Words (because these are really big numbers)	Three billion, three hundred and seventy-one million, one hundred and fifty thousand.	Eight hundred and forty-five million, seven hundred and fifty thousand.

The default fund is holding over three and a quarter billion pounds, whereas the Stewardship counterpart is holding just over a quarter of that amount. Clearly there is an out-and-out winner, but the gap between traditional and ethical investment is closing.

In fact, these figures are constantly growing, and as I edit this chapter towards the beginning of 2025, the latest figures show the Aviva Stewardship Managed fund to have increased by just over £52.8 million. That's over fifty-two million, eight hundred thousand clear tiny messages being sent to Aviva in fund-shaped bottles, of which 2,500 of them were sent by Gemma.

Over the same period, though, the size of the Aviva Managed fund has grown by just over £94.5 million. Obviously this is more, but that's not how any type of growth should be measured.

The following table shows the percentage of growth to the size of each fund between 31/08/2023 and 30/04/2024. To be clear, this refers to growth through the amount of money being invested into the fund rather than the performance of the fund investments themselves:

	Aviva Managed	Aviva Stewardship Managed
Growth in size of fund	2.81%	2.62%*

*Of which, Gemma contributed 0.00030%, rounded to the nearest five decimal places.

Even though the size of the Aviva Managed fund grew by a higher percentage than the Aviva Stewardship Managed fund, the difference is small at 0.19%, which could tell us both or one of the following:

1. There are already a very large number of people looking for ethical investments, actively seeking them out and moving funds into them;
2. Companies offering Workplace Pensions are beginning to use ethical funds as their default fund.

It's hard to know the exact reason, but if either of the above explanations are correct, the trajectory is moving in the right direction. Hopefully, this will prompt Workplace Pension providers to increase the number of ethical funds on offer in pensions. In 2021, the BBC found that there was only one ethical option for every fifteen traditional options in six Workplace Pensions – the others didn't even respond.[1] This feels low, but if demand increases, so will the number of

---

[1] BBC News, 'What's your pension invested in?' (March 2021). https://www.bbc.co.uk/news/business-56170726

WHAT AN ETHICAL FUND TYPICALLY INVESTS IN

ethical options in Workplace Pensions, and slowly, demand is increasing.

~

It's time to get down to the nitty gritty now and find out how the Aviva Stewardship Managed fund is invested. Remember that this is a Stewardship fund, and Stewardship funds set out to change the practices of the companies in which they invest. If we looked at the underlying holdings of the Aviva Stewardship Managed fund and found them to be identical to those of the Aviva Managed fund, it wouldn't necessarily mean that Aviva hasn't held up their end of the deal, but Aviva would have to use the shares held in the Stewardship Managed fund to engage with the relevant companies to influence future decisions. Aviva would have no such commitment with the like-for-like shares in the Aviva Managed fund, though.

As we've already seen, fund managers only publish their top ten holdings, so, like we did with the Aviva Managed fund, let's take a look at what the top ten holdings in the Aviva Stewardship Managed fund are (at the time of writing):[1]

1. 5.1% in *Alphabet Incorporated*: We've come across these before. Alphabet Inc was created through a

---

[1] As before, I would love to add a link to the Factsheet/KIID here, but each time the document is updated, the previous one is removed from the public domain, so any link would become obsolete quickly. I've used the same date as was used for the Aviva Managed fund in Chapter 2 for a fair comparison, and to excuse for the recent uptick in fixed interest holdings in some managed funds.

restructuring of Google. So, it's essentially Google, and it's holding number seven in the traditional Aviva Managed fund.

2. 3.9% in *UnitedHealth Group Incorporated*: An American multinational health services and health-insurance company. According to Investopedia, it's the largest healthcare company in the world[1] and the fifth largest company in the world (both by measured by revenue).[2]

3. 3.8% in *Mastercard Incorporated*: This is tricky one to describe without actually using the word 'Mastercard'. I'd be surprised if you didn't know what Mastercard Inc is if you've ever bought anything, ever. But, on the off chance you've never bought anything, ever, it's an American multinational payment-card service. It's not a bank.

4. 3.6% in *Microsoft Corporation*: I'm using Microsoft right now to write this, so from an ethical standpoint, I guess I'm on board.

5. 3.1% in *VISA*: This is a tricky one to describe without actually using the word 'VISA'. I'd be surprised if you... hang on, I've written something like this already. VISA and Mastercard Inc are not the same, but they do a very similar thing. So, that's 6.9% in card payment services.

---

1 Investopedia, '10 Biggest Healthcare Companies' (June 2024). https://www.investopedia.com/articles/markets/030916/worlds-top-10-health-care-companies-unh-mdt.asp

2 Investopedia, '10 Biggest Companies in the World' (November 2024). https://www.investopedia.com/articles/active-trading/111115/why-all-worlds-top-10-companies-are-american.asp

WHAT AN ETHICAL FUND TYPICALLY INVESTS IN

6. 2.9% in *Elevance Health*: Oh look, another American health-insurance provider. There must be some money in that…
7. 2.9% in *AstraZeneca*: Whilst we were researching what her Aviva Managed fund was invested in (0.9% is in AstraZeneca, if you remember), Gemma has referred to them as the 'stab you in the arm company', but Gemma isn't a fan of needles.
8. 2.7% in *AON*: A British/American consultancy firm specialising in risk management. They're in that slanty 'Cheesegrater' skyscraper in London, which is cool.
9. 2.5% in *Equifax*: An American multinational credit-reporting agency, a bit like Experian, who you may recognise better.
10. 2.4% in *Marsh & McLennan Companies*: A global professional-services company working in risk management, insurance, talent, investment advice, management consulting along with other 'people' stuff.

There is some crossover between this fund and the Aviva Managed Fund, but there's no real reason why we should see too many similarities. Remember, I'm comparing the two funds because they are two funds of a similar risk level available in Gemma's pension. Aviva has never claimed that the Aviva Stewardship Managed fund is the ethical version of the Aviva Managed fund; I'm just using them both due to Gemma's limited options without her transferring.

The first thing I notice on this breakdown of the top ten holdings is that I recognise nearly every company, and the ones I don't are clearly huge. I've met people who choose not to invest in ethical funds because they assume it means their money would be invested in small wind farms, vegan-food companies and hemp tea. I kid you not. I know people who believe that to invest their pension ethically would be to give their money away to hippies who are still living in the sixties. You'll get no judgement from me if you do decide to do that, but this isn't that. These are some of the biggest companies in the world, and they could, and do, show up on any conventional managed fund. Fear of how these funds invest should not stop anyone from investing ethically.

The second thing which stood out to me in this list, though, was the counter of the first point. These *are* huge companies, with a level of stability which is required for a pension fund, but for that reason, they also feel a bit underwhelming. Where are all the renewable-energy companies and exciting ethical start-ups? Maybe I *like* hemp tea and want to help fund its future... Instead, we have two consultancy firms, two health-insurance companies, two payment-card services and a load of tech stock.

If I'd started this whole process by saying to Gemma, 'Do you want to change your pension to invest in the top tech companies, American health-insurance companies and risk-management firms?' I'm sure she'd have said no.

Gemma will read this chapter soon, so I'd best try to explain why the move was worth it... Let's compare the holdings of both funds. In the same way we did for the Aviva Managed fund in Chapter 5, the below table uses the collective value of the Aviva Stewardship Managed fund (£845,750,000) to show how much money is being allocated to the top ten holdings:

WHAT AN ETHICAL FUND TYPICALLY INVESTS IN

Holding	Percentage of fund	Value of investment	Or...*
Alphabet Incorporated	5.1%	£43,133,250	£43.1 million
UnitedHealth Group Incorporated	3.9%	£32,984,250	£33.0 million
Mastercard Incorporated	3.8%	£32,138,500	£32.1 million
Microsoft Corporation	3.6%	£30,447,000	£30.4 million
VISA	3.1%	£26,218,250	£26.2 million
Elevance Health	2.9%	£24,526,750	£24.5 million
AstraZeneca	2.9%	£24,526,750	£24.5 million
AON	2.7%	£22,835,250	£22.8 million
Equifax	2.5%	£21,143,750	£21.1 million
Marsh & McLennan Companies	2.4%	£20,298,000	£20.3 million
Unaccounted for	**67.1%**	**£567,498,250**	**£567.5 million**

*Rounded to the nearest £100,000.

As we've already seen, there are three holdings in the above list which are also held in the Aviva Managed fund. These are *Alphabet Incorporated*, *Microsoft Corporation* and *AstraZeneca*.

The other holdings in the Aviva Managed fund, which don't show up in the Aviva Stewardship Managed fund top ten, are:

- 3.8% in US Treasury 1.123% Index-Linked 01/33
- SPDR ETF Bloomberg Emerging Markets Local Bonds UCITS
- Apple
- UK Treasury Bill 0% 11/12/2023
- Shell
- Amazon.com
- Nestlé S.A

I should stress again that these funds can't necessarily be directly compared. They are, however, the two funds which are the closest in risk level and structure within Gemma's pension, and in fact, they do have the same fund manager. The only defining difference is that one fund is considered ethical.

This is the part of the chapter which will hopefully make Gemma glad she's made the change. The Aviva Stewardship Managed fund does *not* invest more than 2.4% in Nestlé. If you remember, Gemma was unhappy about Nestlé's baby milk scandal in the seventies, and she doesn't love a lot about the Nestlé production chain. It also doesn't invest more than 2.4% in Amazon.com, a company which Gemma feels uncomfortable holding her money with due to worker's rights scandals, and it doesn't invest more than 2.4% in Apple or Shell.

There isn't anything to say that the fund shouldn't invest more than 2.4% in these companies, but at least at the highest level, it doesn't.

Considering the two funds have the same manager, and the same objectives (with the one defining difference of ethics), this is significant. The implication is that these companies have been excluded due to an ethical criterion, or that the fund manager feels that the investors' money held within this fund can more positively impact the chosen holdings than it could Apple, Nestlé, Shell and Amazon.

It's interesting also that Microsoft Corporation and Alphabet Incorporated remain, while Apple has disappeared. I'm not claiming that Apple is unethical in any way, but I am saying that the Aviva fund manager, the person in charge of both funds, finds it less likely that the fund could influence

WHAT AN ETHICAL FUND TYPICALLY INVESTS IN

Apple. This could be for any number of reasons, but they have actively held Apple in the Managed fund and actively dismissed it, at least from the top ten holdings, for the Stewardship fund.

You might be asking why I keep bringing up the 2.4% figure. We can only be sure that Nestlé, Apple, etc. aren't one of the top ten holdings, and the smallest of the top ten holdings is 2.4%. The table still shows a huge amount of investor money is with undisclosed holdings. In fact, 67.1% (£567.5 million) of the Aviva Stewardship Managed fund is undisclosed. That's £1,677.50 of Gemma's £2,500 pension, to give that some relatable perspective.

~

As always, beyond the top ten holdings, the fund is opaque. All we can do is read the ethical criteria and fund documents to get an idea of what's being considered. As I mentioned in the last chapter, funds with the word 'Stewardship' in the name tend to be Stewardship funds – duh. But as I also mentioned in the last chapter, a lot of funds cover more than one type of screening, and the Aviva Stewardship Managed fund is one of them. According to Aviva, this fund has three elements of screening:

1. **Negative Screening:** Aviva say that the Stewardship fund doesn't invest in any of the following: weapons, alcohol, gambling, adult entertainment (by which they mean pornography rather than *Eastenders*), social controversies, thermal coal, oil and gas, nuclear-power generation, genetic modification, concerning chemicals, animal testing, fur, endangered species or environmental

controversies. There are caveats after most of these categories, such as a percentage of turnover which would be allowable to be held in the fund (for example, supermarkets making under 10% turnover from tobacco would be permissible, with a future goal to reduce this percentage).

2. **Positive Screening:** Aviva says the fund invests in companies which make a positive impact to society, and that the investment team use the UN's Sustainable Development Goals as a framework when selecting companies in which to invest. Aviva don't provide much more information on this, but it sounds positive, which I guess makes sense, given the type of screening it is.

3. **Engagement:** This is the stewardship part. Aviva says the fund (along with Aviva's other Stewardship funds) discuss ethical issues with the company chairs of the held investments; they create programmes which help the companies the fund holds shares in improve (currently focusing on single-use plastic and diversity and inclusion in the workplace); and finally, they team up with other stakeholders to drive further change.

As I've said before, there is a certain element of vagueness, because the number of companies a fund holds, and the need to be able to quickly move money if necessary, means it's hard to be incredibly specific, but traditional funds don't have this added layer of care.

Going back to Nestlé: it is possible that Nestlé is held in the fund – but it's perhaps unlikely due to the fund's negative screening of social controversies and animal testing. Nestlé hasn't adopted the UN's Sustainable Development Goals yet, but it has set targets, and the fund only commits to using the goals as a framework, so whilst this could rule the company out, it's not a straight guarantee.

Honestly, I couldn't tell you for sure, but given these three points, I'd be surprised if the fund holds shares in Nestlé, or Amazon, or Shell.

But I could be wrong. We simply cannot know. But we can know that all these factors are being taken into consideration, and that has to be better than not…

Gemma, that is why you've made a fund switch in your pension.

Reader, if you ever appoint me as your financial adviser, please don't expect reports to be this long. Gemma gets special treatment.

CHAPTER 10

Breaking myths
(like Breaking Bad, *but better)*

This chapter is going to be completely badass. You're going to watch how an average financial adviser like me turned into 'the one who knocks'. Except, unlike Walter White, I'll be knocking myths on the head. Not doors. No drugs. Actual myths. I think you'll agree that this chapter will be better than *Breaking Bad*.

Probably more gripping, if anything.

Myth one
Ethical investments have not performed as well as traditional investments

I hear this one a lot, and it doesn't just come from nowhere, but it is a little outdated. There was a time around twenty years ago when ethical investments were a reasonably new concept for the mainstream, and the performance just didn't match up.

The firm I work for now started as an ethical investment wealth management arm, but when they started, they found it hard to create portfolios of funds which could match up with their traditional counterparts for performance. Now we have both traditional and ethical portfolios and the ethical portfolios more than match up.

In fact, over the past decade they've performed better than the traditional portfolios.

This is down to a few things. Firstly, there are specific targets set by governments for companies to meet from an ethical standpoint. For example, the UK has a target to increase the amount of renewable energy it uses as a percentage of the total energy we use. In simple terms, companies working towards this target should grow, which will grow the funds holding shares in these companies.

Another reason ethical funds have performed well over the past decade is because, increasingly, more people know about them and use them, which raises investment for the companies, allowing them to grow even further. It's like a snowball rolling down a hill, except on a graph the momentum would be upward, not downward.

There are other reasons too, but you shouldn't just take my word for it, and Gemma certainly didn't, so I've compared the growth of the two Aviva funds we've been looking at, with all the data taken from Aviva's own Key Investors Information Document and presented it in a table below. It must feel strange being married to someone who answers so many questions with data tables:

Fund	1 year*	3 years*	5 years*	10 years*
Aviva Managed	8.32%	4.90%	23.95%	62.48%
Aviva Stewardship Managed	10.08%	5.61%	37.96%	124.38%

*Periods up to 30/04/2024 (i.e. '1 year' refers to the period 01/05/2023 to 30/04/2024).

I'd feel uncomfortable if I didn't do the typical financial adviser stuff here, so after I showed Gemma this table, I told her that:

- Nothing is guaranteed
- Investments go down as well as up
- Past performance is not a guarantee of future results.

And they say that romance is dead.

The figures in the table clearly show that the ethical fund has performed better than the non-ethical fund. Aviva has assigned them both the same 'sector average' and they have the same risk level, so in that respect it is a fair comparison.

I'm not saying that the Aviva Stewardship fund is the fund for you, it's just the one that was available in Gemma's pension, and it suited her. There are lots of ethical funds out there which are similar, certainly in most Workplace Pensions, and when I compared the performance of the two funds, I sort of knew which one would be shown favourably, because these funds are both very run of the mill, and it's been this way for the past decade. There's a similar story to be told in the Nest pension – see Chapter 5.

It could go backwards – ethical investments might begin to underperform their traditional counterparts – but don't forget that most ethical funds are still holding some of the biggest companies in the world – it's not wacky hippy stuff – so there is no real reason why they would.

As always, I like to convert things into pizzas, so the next table assumes that Gemma had her £2,500 in a pension ten years ago, and compares what she would have now if she invested in each fund:

Fund	After 10 years Gemma would have...
Aviva Managed	£4,062
Aviva Stewardship Managed	£5,610

If Gemma had invested her £2,500 into the Aviva Managed fund ten years ago, she would now be able to afford 162 takeaways (324 individual pizzas, with garlic mayo, obviously).

If Gemma had invested her £2,500 into the Aviva Stewardship Managed fund ten years ago, she would be able to afford 224 takeaways (448 individual pizzas, with garlic mayo, obviously). That's an additional 124 individual pizzas with garlic mayo. When you annualise that, it equates to an additional 12 pizzas a year gained over the ten-year-period, which is one a month – which, if not informative in any kind of useful way, is certainly pleasing.

Myth two
Ethical investment is too young for us to fully understand

People don't like change. If it ain't broke, don't fix it, right? I tend to agree with this. I rarely buy one of the new variations on a KitKat (with the Chunky being the obvious exception – heady days) and I would NEVER change my pizza provider, but I also agree with the lesser-known phrase: if it is broke, fix it.

To invest ethically is not to invest stupidly. Most ethical funds tend to hold similar company shares to traditional investments but filter them one way or another to ensure that the holdings are both good from a performance perspective *and* from an ethical standpoint. They tweak traditional investments to reward companies that are making the effort without compromising the individual investor (that's you).

It's true that we have over two hundred years of data when it comes to traditional investment and just over fifty years of data when it comes to ethical investing, but the actual companies the funds are holding don't differ that wildly. Any fund could hold shares in a new company, and that would lead to more variables than the nature of the fund itself, so really the only new element here is the concept of screening (whichever method the fund adopts), not the investments themselves.

It's true that people don't like change, but this really isn't that big a change – it's just a tweak to make things better, and that can't be a bad thing.

Myth three
Ethical funds are risky

Just like with the other myths in this chapter, this hasn't stemmed from nowhere. It isn't quite the horror show it sounds, though. Some people seem to think that ethical investment is risky because they'll be putting all their money in new eco technology which might not be the future it thinks it is.

Some people are sceptic of electric cars, choosing not to make the switch from petrol to electric in case electric cars are a thing of the past in the next decade. In the same way, there are people holding off from making the move to ethical investing in case it simply doesn't work. Maybe it's all a bit faddy.

But the thing is, even if the mainstream ethical funds were all invested in electric cars, they would also be invested in other sectors, and the fund managers would make changes to the underlying shares if it seemed like hydrogen-powered cars were likely to take over anytime soon, so that isn't where the risk lies.

No, the additional risk with ethical funds lies somewhere much less exciting – it's in the diversification. If you negatively screen for a particular sector – tobacco, for example – that's one less sector which can be used to diversify the fund. The fewer sectors a fund holds, the lower the level of diversification, and the lower the level of diversification, the higher the risk.

Using the two Aviva funds to illustrate this, the top ten holdings of the Aviva Managed fund accounts for 13.8% of the fund's total holdings, whereas the top ten holdings of the Aviva Stewardship Managed fund accounts for 32.9% of the fund's total holdings. This is because the Aviva Stewardship fund has an ethical criterion which, whilst still allowing the fund to invest in huge multinational conglomerates, restricts which ones it can invest in. Simply speaking, the fund invests in fewer companies, which is likely to make it more volatile.

So, it isn't the *nature* of the companies in which ethical funds invest which increases the level of risk, it's the *number*, and hopefully that makes the whole thing a bit less scary.

Myth four
Ethical funds are more expensive

Not always, but yeah, this one's basically true. There's more work in managing an ethical fund, because the fund managers have the extra element of research in the screening process, and that costs a bit more money. It isn't normally much, and over the past decade, at least, the performance of many ethical funds has far outweighed the additional cost.

~

You think I believe these myths? I am not the believer. No. I am the one who knocks. (Knocks these myths on the head, that is.)

See, I told you that this chapter was going to be completely badass.

And just like that, boom, you're binge reading the next chapter…

CHAPTER 11

Greenwashing

When I told my mate I was writing a book about how to make your finances more ethical, his first reaction was disheartening, to say the least.

'Mate, no one is going to read that.'

Well, you and I know this simply isn't true. Here you are on Chapter 11, binge reading since the chapter about breaking myths.

The second thing my mate said was something I'd heard many times before: 'It's all pointless anyway – it's all greenwashing.'

As a part of my job, I suggest the idea of ethical investment to clients who have never thought about it before. Not always, but often, this idea of it all being pointless due to greenwashing comes up.

It's a valid concern to bring up, so instead of telling my mate to wind his neck in, I decided to carry out a little research and write a chapter about it.

But it's a chapter which I guess he'll never read.

~

My personal stance on greenwashing is that yes, of course it happens, but I don't think it should stop genuine progression.

I'm sceptical of any big-brand fashion retailer making sustainable fashion claims, and companies which have a green label on their packaging all of a sudden makes me cringe. Coca-Cola did this with Coca-Cola Life (worth a Google if you're into greenwashing stories), but ultimately, they got called out and it's off the shelves now.

Similarly, McDonald's brought out paper straws in a show of attempting to reduce plastic pollution, but it turned out that these straws were non-recyclable anyway.

All very negative stuff, and of course big-brand fashion, Coca-Cola and McDonald's have contributed to people being more sceptical of genuine ethical moves. In an attempt to counter this, I'll put my own positive spin on these examples of greenwashing:

- Any retailers making sustainable fashion claims are, if nothing else, drawing attention to the need for sustainable fashion and the benefit of individuals wearing clothes for as long as possible before replacing them. I first became aware of the pitfalls of fast fashion through news stories of big companies attempting to tackle it. Now, the big brands may have been making false claims, but I do believe this has at least driven awareness in individuals and younger fashion start-ups to make genuine changes.
- Coca-Cola was called out on its 'Life' product, leading to bad press, and, to my mind, heightened public awareness of the health issues with Coca-Cola in general – look, maybe I'm wrong, but I do like to find the positive in things.
- McDonald's made a big point of converting to paper straws. We now know that they weren't recyclable and

didn't directly contribute to a reduction of material pollution, but they did highlight the huge issue of one-use plastics. I'd be surprised if this didn't have some sort of effect on the smaller companies with more of a conscience looking to make genuine changes.

I'm aware that these are some very positive spins on some very dubious corporate actions, but as I've already mentioned, I tend to be annoyingly positive.

My point is that we as a public can decide that every positive move a company makes is simply greenwashing and not buy in, or we can accept that there will be mistakes along the way, and while there are certainly 'bad guys' in the corporate world, remember there are also 'good guys' too.

For me, the biggest issue with greenwashing isn't that, for example, the straws aren't recyclable, it's the contributing factor it has on a growing mistrust in anything attempting to be ethical. As soon as the consumer writes every positive change off as 'greenwashing', there will be no genuine positive change.

With this in mind, let's revisit the link between greenwashing and ethical investment. I want to find out if these news stories of non-recyclable straws are relevant to ethical investing, or if the scepticism of ethical investing is a result of public opinion on greenwashing and nothing more.

As an aside, when I became more aware of the pitfalls of fast fashion, I made a more conscious effort to buy fewer clothes, but found that I never bought any new clothes anyway. It's the reason I wear a suit to work. If I wore my normal clothes to meetings, I wouldn't have any clients. I have two looks in my wardrobe – smart and homeless.

~

The big difference between a company such as McDonald's and an ethical fund is that McDonald's is one company, and an ethical fund is a collection of investments into several different companies.

Let's say you invest in a fund that negatively screens for investments in the sex industry, and which holds McDonald's Corp shares. First off, holding shares in McDonald's Corp is completely fine for this fund manager. McDonald's do not, as far as I'm aware, deal in the sex industry.

The underlying company (in this case McDonald's) could easily be the perpetrator of greenwashing, but it is not the fund manager's responsibility to control the underlying companies. It is their responsibility to either influence them or vet them. In this example, McDonald's bringing out non-recyclable straws and claiming they are recyclable would not automatically mean the holding in the company would be dropped from the fund. The screening process (ensuring no investment in the sex industry) has not been breached, but as we saw in earlier chapters, lots of ethical funds do a 'catch-all' in order to gather as much investment as possible, so some form of action may be taken.

If you're holding a Stewardship fund, the manager may decide to focus on influencing future decisions made by McDonald's Corp, or they may just decide to sell the McDonald's Corp shares. If you're holding a positively or negatively screened fund, there is also a good chance that the shares would be sold, and the same would likely happen in a best-in-class fund.

From a top-down view, investing in an ethical fund is a way of holding companies accountable for their actions. The wrong moves could lead to a large divestment for the underlying company, so from this point of view at least, investing in an ethical fund goes some way to counter greenwashing at a company level.

But who is holding the funds and the fund managers themselves accountable?

Actually, that's a massive question – let's turn it into a subtitle…

Who is holding the funds and the fund managers themselves accountable?

The SFDR and SDR.

You're with me when I say 'the SFDR and SDR', right? No? OK, well one stands for the Sustainable Finance Disclosure Regulation, and is relevant to the EU market, and the other stands for Sustainable Disclosure Requirements, and is relevant to UK markets.

You're still not clear? No, I wasn't either. They don't make this stuff easy. Let's break it down.

Both the SFDR and the SDR were put in place with the specific aim of tackling greenwashing in the industry and to help investors make more informed decisions. There is a lot of talk of transparency and accountability in the papers and marketing, and it all sounds generally good, but let's look a little closer.

The SFDR (the European one)

The SFDR was put in place first, back in March 2021,[1] and it categorises investments in three main categories, which are:

- **Article 6:** An investment with no sustainable focus;
- **Article 8:** Investments which promote positive environmental and social qualities;
- **Article 9:** Investments with distinct sustainability objectives where the majority of the holdings are ESG focused.

Fund managers are required to use several sets of criteria (the United Nations' Sustainable Development Goals, for example) to show under which article the investment sits, and then make that information publicly available to investors.

You're likely to come across these articles being advertised by funds when you're doing your own research, so I've included them here, and they do remain relevant, but we're no longer in the EU, so the SDR is the one we need to pay the most attention to.

The SDR (the UK one)

First up, let's just congratulate the Financial Conduct Authority (FCA) on coming up with an exciting twist on the

---

1 EUR-Lex, *Regulation (EU) 2019/2088 of the European Parliament and of the Council of 27 November 2019 on sustainability-related disclosures in the financial services sector* (January 2024).
https://eur-lex.europa.eu/legal-content/EN/TXT/?uri=CELEX:32019R2088

name. The SDR final rules were published in November 2023,[1] and again, it categorises investments in three main categories (plus a mixed one), which this time are:

- **Sustainability Focus:** An investment with at least 70% of assets in environmentally and/or socially sustainable holdings;
- **Sustainability Improvers:** An investment with at least 70% of assets which have the potential to improve environmental and/or social sustainability over time (a 'stewardship' fund would fall into this category);
- **Sustainability Impact:** An investment with at least 70% of assets aiming to make a specific and measurable impact on an environmental and/or social outcome;
- **Sustainability Mixed Goals:** An investment which holds a combination of two or more of the other two labels (I suspect that Gemma's new Aviva fund will fall into this category, as there is an element of stewardship, but also positive and negative screening going on).

Labels became available in July 2024 and are voluntary, so it's very new and we're yet to see how it will look in reality, but what is clear is that the FCA (another catchy name) are taking greenwashing seriously, and that fund managers will be held accountable to their claims.

Add to this that there is a blanket 'anti-greenwashing rule' in the paper, and I'm personally convinced that

---

[1] FCA, *Policy Statement PS23/16: Sustainability Disclosure Requirements (SDR) and investment labels* (November 2023).
https://www.fca.org.uk/publication/policy/ps23-16.pdf

moving my family's money into ethical investment is the right thing to do.

But that's just me. It's up to you to decide what is right for you.

~

I'm not saying greenwashing in ethical investment doesn't happen. It does, otherwise the SFDR and SDR wouldn't be needed to tackle it, but I still believe that the term 'greenwashing' deters people from trying, and that it negatively impacts real positive change in the world.

I don't want the fear of greenwashing to stop me from at least trying to do what I think is right.

As for my mate, if he reads this chapter then maybe I'll have changed his mind on greenwashing with ethical investment. I'll send him a copy of this book when it's done. He'll tell me when I next see him that he's read it even if he hasn't, but I'll know if he's telling the truth or not, for one very simple reason…

Greg, mate, I think you have very nice hair and I wish my barnet was as full as yours.

He'll definitely bring that up.

CHAPTER 12

What you can do (pensions)

Gemma works in marketing, and whilst this book doesn't make a good case for working in marketing from a retirement perspective (£2,500 anyone?), it should probably follow marketing conventions, because it's trying to convince you to do something specific.

'You need a call to action,' Gemma told me after reading the rest of the book.

'What do you mean?' I asked. 'Did you not read the pizza chat? People will *want* to make changes to their pensions and investments, if just for the extra 124 individual pizzas (with garlic mayo, obviously) they might get after ten years.'

'What do you actually want your readers to do?' she asked, rudely ignoring my valid point.

I looked deep into her eyes, and with a passion I hope has come through in this book, I answered, 'Change,' as poignantly as I could manage. 'I want readers to change their pensions, and make the right investments, and bank with the right banks. I want readers – nay, I want *all* people – to know how to be financially stable in themselves, and in the process use their money to improve the world. I want to turn this planet into a place our children can be proud to call their home, through investment and pensions.'

'If that's what you want,' she said, somewhat dubious looking, 'you need to stop writing long superfluous paragraphs, and tell them what to do, and be more specific than just saying "Change".'

'Fine,' I said, 'I will,' and I have.

First, pensions.

You may remember in Chapter 2 we looked at the two main types of pension – Defined Contribution and Defined Benefit. Hopefully you now know which one of these two types of pension you have, and you probably have a good idea of what you can do with it, but to summarise... I mean, to call you to action:

Defined Contribution

This is an area with huge scope for positive change, and you can be a part of that. To recap, we broke Defined Contribution pensions down into two categories – Workplace Pension and Personal Pension.

Let's look at Workplace Pensions first:

Workplace Pensions

If you have a job, you're likely (but not guaranteed) to have a Workplace Pension. If you and your employer are still paying money into this pension, it's unlikely you'd want to move it to a different pension provider, because you might lose all that lovely free money. So how do you make your existing Workplace Pension ethical without moving the pension itself?

WHAT YOU CAN DO (PENSIONS)

Step 1: Find a list of the available funds. Remember, if you've never actively looked at the pension yourself, you'll be invested in the default fund. You'll find a list of the funds available to you by either logging on to your pension online, or by phoning your pension provider and requesting one. Most Workplace Pension providers offer between nine and 140 funds. They generally have an online list of the available funds, with the KIIDs/factsheets available on the same page.

Step 2: Create a shortlist. Most Workplace Pension providers make a point of showing which funds they consider ethical. If you're trying to keep things simple, you're looking for funds with the following words in the fund names:

- Sustainable
- Responsible
- Ethical
- Socially responsible
- Stewardship
- Future (though this is also used in some traditional funds, so double check the KIID/factsheet)

Step 3.1: Select the fund, or funds, which meet your personal ethical requirements. To do this, you need to read the KIIDs/factsheets on your shortlist of funds. Check for an ethical statement. You now know the different type of ethical investments available and should be able to decipher what it all means. Are you looking for a screened fund, or a Stewardship fund? Most Workplace Pensions offer a mixed option. You might find that there is only one ethical fund available in your pension, but remember, as long as you have a Workplace Pension which your employer is paying into, you don't want to transfer to a different provider, because you might lose the employer contributions. What's best for you personally should come before your fund selection.

Step 3.2: Write to your pension provider. This step is only relevant if you can't find a suitable ethical fund. If there are no ethical funds available in your Workplace Pension at all, you can request one, and if you're after a specific type of fund which you can't find, you can request it. Be prepared to be disappointed, but pressure on the providers in itself is progress. Let these providers know what we want.

The lovely people at Make My Money Matter, which focuses specifically on climate action in finance, have made this incredibly easy, by using their 'contact your pension provider' page, here:

https://makemymoneymatter.co.uk/pensions

What do we want? Suitable ethical funds. When do we want it? Well, now, but we appreciate there is normally an eight-week turnaround period on these things.

Now that's a catchy chant.

Step 4: Check the risk, performance and fees of your chosen fund/s. I can't tell you what is right for you here, but obviously you want a good return for the right amount of risk, and it's important that you know what you're paying into your pension.

Step 5: TAKE ACTION! Sorry for shouting, but it's an important step. You can either log in to your pension and make the fund switch online, which is normally the easiest option, or you could call your provider to request the fund switch. Make a point of checking that all future contributions will also be invested in the new fund.

Step 6: Additional step for absolute pension legends. If the default fund in your pension is not an ethical fund, why not write to your employer asking them to consider changing their selected default fund. If enough people did this, and your employer made the change, every new employee joining the scheme would be invested in at least some form of ethical fund, without even having to do anything. That way, if any of the future employees ever marry a financial adviser, that financial adviser might not write a whole book about it. I reckon the employee would thank you for that.

Step 7: Sit back with a cup of tea, knowing you've done good. Or coffee, or juice, or water, or absinth, or whatever floats your boat. Maybe get a pizza or a Kit-Kat. You did something worthwhile today, and you should acknowledge that.

~

It really is as simple as that if you have a Workplace Pension. If you hold a Personal Pension, there are added steps, but generally you'll find you have more choices:

Personal Pensions

I'm going to include paid-up Workplace Pensions in this category, meaning if you had a Defined Contribution pension with a previous employer which isn't receiving employer contributions any more, this bit will be relevant to you. It's also relevant if you happen to hold a Defined Contribution pension which you set up yourself.

There are two simple routes to making ethical changes in your Personal Pension, and which one you choose will depend heavily on how much research you're willing to take on.

There is the easy route which takes the same steps as making changes to a Workplace Pension, which we've just gone through. If you take this option, don't do Step 3.2. though, because if you can't find a fund in the Personal Pension you hold which you want to invest in, rather than write off to the provider, you can just move your pension to a different provider.[1]

If you can't find a suitable fund in your pension, or if you just want to be completely thorough and take the slightly harder route, you can follow the below steps:

Step 1: Search for the right fund for you, anywhere. Some Personal Pension providers can hold almost any UK regulated fund, which means that if there is nothing stopping you from transferring your pension to a different one, you can invest in any fund you like. There are a couple of websites that allow you to filter funds for different ethical purposes and criteria, but I've copied a personal favourite, SRI Services, here:

https://www.sriservices.co.uk/

---

[1] That's unless there are guarantees or benefits specific to the pension which you already have – if you're not sure about this, you probably do need an adviser. I'm sorry you got this far in the book to find that out.

SRI services allow you to filter the type of product you want to search (pension, in this case), and then filter for what is important to you. It provides a list of funds that fulfil your criteria, with a link to more information on each fund.

Step 2: Check the risk, performance and fees of your chosen fund/s. As before, this part will be personal to you, but you want a good return relative to the risk, and you need to know what you're paying in fees.

Step 3: Find the right provider. Maybe the provider you already use offers the fund or funds you want to invest in, in which case, happy days – you can move on to Step 4. If it doesn't, you need to find a provider that does. This takes a little bit of research – the term 'open architecture' refers to a provider that offers funds by fund managers other than themselves. Google 'open architecture personal pensions' and check which ones offer the fund or funds you want to invest in. Once you have a shortlist, you need to compare the costs of the providers and their general customer experience (i.e. which one has the best online functionality). This step may take a while, but you'll probably hold your pension for the rest of your life, or at least until retirement, so it's worth putting the time in now.

Step 4: TAKE ACTION! I really must stop shouting like that. If you're changing provider, you create a new Personal Pension with the new provider and then request the transfer through the new provider. Normally it's a very straightforward process on the provider website, but it can still take several weeks to happen. If it isn't obvious how to do it online, you can call the new provider, and they can lend you a hand. Once your money is with the correct provider, new or existing, you just need to select the fund or funds you want to invest in and action it. Again, if it isn't clear online, you can call the provider, and they should help you. If they don't help you, you probably did Step 3 wrong.

Step 5: Sit back with a cup of tea, knowing you've done good. No, actually, get a couple. You deserve it.

~

These steps cannot be a catch-all for everyone, but they are the basic steps you can take to make sure your pension is invested ethically. There are a few exceptions – maybe your pension has guarantees attached which you'd lose if you moved it to a different provider. If you think this might be the case, ask the provider, or maybe even look for advice. Also, if your pension is massive (for starters, how are you this far into the book? You should have sought advice after reading the introduction) you may want to look for lots of different funds rather than just the one or two.

Now for Defined Benefit pensions. You may remember in Chapter 2 I said wouldn't talk too much about these, so if we're joining you here straight from Chapter 2 because this is the type of pension you have, hi! You've missed a lot of talk about pizza.

Defined Benefit

If you have a Defined Benefit pension, you don't have any real control over the money the scheme holds. What you own is the promise of a guaranteed income in retirement, so there's very little you can do to 'ethical it up'.

All liability lies with the scheme, so ultimately it is up to the scheme how to invest the underlying money, but here is what you *can* do:

Step 1: Request an investment remit or ethical statement. If you have a public sector Defined Benefit pension you may well be provided with an investment remit. If you hold a private sector Defined Benefit pension, you're likely to hit a brick wall. You should still try, but just be prepared for disappointment.

Step 2: Write to your scheme and campaign. This is all you can do, but you'd be surprised how effective it can be. A representative from Make My Money Matter told me they've had feedback from pension schemes to suggest that it only takes a few hundred messages from pension members to make a change to the way the fund is run. There are so few people making the effort to write in that the ones who do have a huge impact. Adding to the discussion, a representative at Brunel Pension Partnership told me that every message and request gets actioned and discussed because they are working on behalf of the member (you). Be one of those people making the effort. It has more impact than you think, and if the underlying investments are changed, the amount of money which you'll have helped move into ethical holdings will be huge.

~

'How's that for a call to action?' I asked Gemma.

'It's good,' she replied, but what about investments?'

'Aha,' I said, 'well, you see, the next chapter is called…'

CHAPTER 13

What you can do
(regular, run-of-the-mill investments)

For me and my family, this section refers to what we could do with our six-year-old's money. I'm going to run you through the steps I took to invest his money ethically, because I think that might help you, but first I'll run you through the steps he took.

Step 1: Read *Oi Dog!*

Step 2: Kick a football at the sofa over and over again.

Step 3: Tell your dad you've scored a hat-trick every three kicks.

Step 4: Fall asleep, but only after hearing five stories and drinking three cups of milk.

Step 5: Wake up. Hey presto, you're invested in a sensible and ethical manner.

We didn't tell my son it had even happened, partly because he'd want to spend it all on football cards now, and partly because it was 2 a.m. when he woke up. Honestly, I think if it was down to him, it would never have happened.

Here are the steps Gemma and I took to invest his money ethically during those few hours in which he was asleep.

Step 1: Search for the right fund for you. For me and Gemma, this meant working out how we wanted our son's money invested. It meant embodying the mind of a sensible six-year-old, which is hard because in real life sensible six-year-olds don't exist. Maybe you're investing for your kids, or maybe you're investing for yourself. Either way, once you know what you want (maybe using Chapters 7 and 8 to help you), I'd direct you to a website like this one where you can filter for the type of ethical investment you want:

https://www.sriservices.co.uk/

Step 2: Check the risk, performance and fees of your chosen fund/s. As always, you must check these things and make sure they're right for you. If you've found lots of funds that meet your requirements, you can use risk, performance and fees to directly compare them to find the right one.

Step 3: Find the right product. Unlike with a pension, you need to find the right type of product in which to invest the money. You could consider a stocks and shares ISA, a General Investment Account (GIA) or even open a pension. There are benefits and pitfalls to each product, so check online which you think is the right one for you.

Step 4: Find the right provider. Find a provider that allows you to hold the fund or funds you've chosen to invest in. Let's say you've decided to invest in a stocks and shares ISA, for example – you might Google 'best stocks and shares ISA' and then check through your results to find the providers that offer the relevant funds. You could also use Moneysavingexpert.com or similar comparison sites to do this. Once you have a shortlist, you need to compare the costs of the providers and their general customer experience (i.e. which one has the best online functionality).

Step 5: TAKE ACTION! Open the relevant account with your chosen product online, select the fund or funds you've chosen, and action the investment. I've made it sound simple because it is. The work is in Steps 1 to 4. Step 5 is easy, and if it isn't, you should revisit Step 4.

Step 6: Sit back with a cup of tea, knowing you've done good. I can't stress this one enough. It's as important as the other steps. Look after yourself – you're one of the good ones.

~

I mentioned football cards earlier. Just to emphasise the power of regular investing, if you were to invest the cost of a pack of football cards (£2.50) every week into an investment (an ethical one, naturally), after eighteen years, assuming the money grew by 5% each year, you'd have £3,754. That's an additional £1,414 over the £2,340 you'd have paid in. You get six football cards in a pack, so that's 9,009 individual football cards.

On the flip side, if you just bought a pack of football cards every week for eighteen years, you'd only end up with 5,616 football cards (though, admittedly you'd have a new pack of football cards every week).

I asked my six-year-old which he'd prefer, and his answer was... well, let's just say it wasn't in the spirit of the book.

Football cards can't buy you a car when you're eighteen, though, can they, kiddo?

CHAPTER 14

What you can do (banking)

As we discussed in Chapter 4, this is one of the quickest and easiest ways to make sure your money is held in the right place from an ethical point of view. Having now confessed, it brings no end of joy to Gemma that I wasn't banking ethically, especially after I've been referring to her as the Pension Gangster for several months.

The most ethical banks in the UK are the ones which advertise themselves as being ethical. It's that simple. The big banks – the massive names we've all grown up with – don't talk much about their lending criteria because, as we've already seen, not enough people are asking. This is likely to change over the next decade as awareness grows and pressure builds, but at the moment, despite various campaigns (often around sponsorship of an event), the big banks continue to lend to big fossil-fuel companies, for example.

The steps here are pretty basic, but the impact you can make with your money by following them, and the message you will send to the big-name banks, is huge.

Step 1: Research the bank. I Googled 'ethical banks' and came up with a list of the top five from Choose.co.uk. Triodos come out on top. Triodos were top on Moneysavingexpert.com too, and they were high on the

Ethicalconsumer.org list of current accounts. I've researched this for clients over the years, and Triodos tend to consistently find themselves at the top of various lists, largely due to a refusal to invest in fossil-fuel projects, preferring to focus on renewable energy. Other banks which featured on most lists included Staling, Monzo and Ecology Building Society.

Step 2: Check your chosen provider offers the type of account you want. For me, this was a current account and an instant-access cash ISA. You're probably just looking for the accounts you already hold with your current bank.

Step 3: Check rates. This is less necessary for a current account, as most people hold small amounts of money in their current account, but for savings accounts this is more important. There are good rates out there, but you probably won't find the absolute best rate on the market in one of the ethical banks. To put this into perspective, find out the rate offered by your chosen ethical bank, and then check the available rates offered by what we'll call non-ethical banks, and calculate the monetary difference you'd get over a year. It might also be worth factoring in any freebies or loyalty bonuses that your current bank might be offering you. Then decide what means the most to you: the monetary difference (for me it was £75 for the first year) or any ethical impact you might want to have.

Step 4: TAKE ACTION! Open your chosen bank account/s and request a transfer. This is normally online and is much easier than you'd imagine. All direct debits are transferred automatically and you're sent a new card. You really don't have to do anything once you've requested the transfer.

Step 5: Sit back with a cup of tea, knowing you've done good. You, my friend, are an absolute gem. If you've carried out every step listed in Chapters 12, 13 *and* 14, then you deserve more than a cup of tea. Maybe take that new bank card of yours and treat yourself to a bag of chips.

CHAPTER 15

My wife, the pension goddess

Here we are, at the end of the book, and just to check if he's still reading:

Greg, mate, I still have your Offspring CD – let me know if you want it back.

Even if Greg isn't still reading, you're here, and that means more to me anyway – I've always liked you. I really hope this book has inspired you to make some financial changes, however small.

This journey started as a quick chat between Gemma and I one evening after our six-year-old had eventually fallen asleep, about how to invest some money on his behalf.

It escalated, to say the least.

~

So where are we now? Well, as I indicated at the beginning of the book, my son now invests his money globally, in several different asset classes and across a variety of companies and institutions.

It is only in the one fund, though, so it's not as complicated as it first sounds. Gemma and I make regular payments to his savings, which get invested into the fund we chose for him.

The fund in question doesn't invest in gambling, tobacco, pornography, the sex industry or armaments. We know that because the fund literature (KIID/factsheet) tells us so. Now that we've done our research we don't need to keep checking it. If the ethical statement changes, we'll be told via email well in advance of the changes taking place. There is a leaning towards renewable energy, but we haven't opted to exclude fossil fuels entirely, preferring to find a fund with an element of stewardship to its approach.

I'm not going to tell you which fund my six-year-old is invested in. As I've said before, ethics is a personal thing, and I think it's important for people to do their own research. Maybe you'll come out with the same fund as my six-year-old, or maybe you'll come out with a different one, but the one you find will be the one for you, not me, and not him.

My six-year-old isn't going to tell you which fund he's invested in either, by the way, because he literally has no idea about it. He can read now, and there will no doubt be copies of this book lying around the house when it's done. Am I worried he's going to read any of them?

Haha, based on how often he does his homework? No. No, I am not.

~

What became of the OPG (Original Pension Gangster)? Happily, I didn't lose her to the thug life of traditional retirement investing. No longer is she wrapped up in a life of (investing in) guns, alcohol and pornography. She's off the mean streets of the Aviva Managed fund, and on the path to recovery in the self-righteous Aviva Stewardship Managed fund.

It sounds like nothing, and administratively it was nothing, but at the same time it's everything. It's £17.50 taken away from Nestlé and £20 taken away from Shell. It's £2,500 going towards influencing the big decisions being made by multinational companies, and it's a message to the world of fund managers that this is what matters to investors.

For Gemma, it's peace of mind. She's doing everything she can with the limited funds she has to make a real change in the world.

It's very powerful, but if none of that feels important enough to you, it is also, potentially, 124 more individual pizzas (with garlic mayo, obviously) in retirement.

Unlike with my son's investment, I've made it clear which fund Gemma has ended up investing in. More than clear – I've written several chapters about it, but that doesn't make it the right fund for you. Gemma's pension offered only thirty funds, and it just so happened that one of them offered a level of ethical investing which Gemma was happy with. If she'd moved providers, her choice of fund could have been much greater, but for Gemma that wasn't necessary.

Gemma never wanted to be a pension gangster. She became one because her then employer made decisions on her behalf. She didn't take action, because, well, no one ever does.

Now she has taken action, but not only with the money in her own pension. Gemma's written to her ex-employer to ask them to change the default fund in the pension scheme. I don't know if they'll do much with an email from an ex-employee, but it will bring the idea to the front of at least one person's mind when they open the email, and that could well be the start. Maybe Gemma is the hundredth person to write an email to the company. Maybe hers will be the email which cements a final decision for them.

The point is, Gemma can sleep well knowing that she's done everything she can – though she should probably also buy a bamboo toothbrush. Did I mention my bamboo toothbrush? It's a very popular conversation piece at parties.

I think.

It's been a while since I was invited to a party.

~

There are no prizes for guessing how I've changed my own personal banking. I now bank with Triodos. There was no dramatic moment where I got to strut into my local HSBC and shout out that I would be leaving them, destined for more ethical pastures and that's a shame really, because that might have convinced other people to do the same thing.

I guess I could still do that.

The most important thing to know about our banking now, though, is that Gemma was never with Triodos in the first place. She keeps her money with one of the other banks which pops up on all the various lists of ethical banks, but it isn't number one on any of them.

If you take one thing away from this book, let it be that I bank more ethically than Gemma. I've bought it up every day since I transferred the accounts, and our marriage is all the stronger for it. Probably.

~

You may have noticed that at the beginning of this chapter, I changed Gemma's title from 'Pension Gangster' to 'Pension Goddess'. I was particularly proud of the change and knew she would be too.

'Pension goddess,' I called up the stairs, 'oh, pension goddess…'

Gemma didn't reply.

'Pension goddess?' I called once more before eventually getting a response.

'What? I'm sorting the washing.'

'I'm calling you pension goddess instead of pension gangster,' I shouted, excitedly.

'Can't you just call me Gemma?' she replied.

'Oh,' I said, a bit deflated. 'Well, I've just finished writing the book, so, I guess I can, yes.'

ACKNOWLEDGEMENTS

One night, after reading a book about elephants, my son asked if I could write a non-fiction book. I'm an absolute sucker for that kid and tend to do whatever he says, which is how we've ended up here, in the acknowledgements of my first non-fiction book.

With his request in mind, alongside a new novel, I started working on *Pension Gangster* (which at that time was just called *Non-Fiction Book*). I showed Gemma the introduction to *Pension Gangster* and at the same time showed her the first chapter of the new novel.

'You know,' she said, 'I think people will want the ethical finance book. It's a bit different, but I think it's worth writing.' Never has someone said 'This novel is rubbish' in such a kind way.

If it wasn't for Gemma and Indy, this book wouldn't exist, so thank you both for nudging me in the right direction, but also for being the perfect family that you are.

Writing *Pension Gangster* has not been a lonely experience. I've had constant support and help from Matthew Barrett (who has a doctorate in Ethical Investment Management Technique but is too humble to ever mention it) and the rest of the team at Churchill Wealth Management.

I'm grateful also to Oliver Wright from Brunel Pension Partnership for his invaluable help on how large background investment for Defined Benefit schemes can work.

Thank you to David Hayman, Tony Burdon and Izzy Howden from Make My Money Matter for providing both feedback and the cover quote.

Thank you to Frances Quinn who kindly read and provided feedback on the entire manuscript, and to all the D20 authors (we all had our debut books published during lockdown in 2020, hence the name), who are always on hand for support during the writing and publishing process.

My friends Chris Dean and Becky Goodall were kind enough to read *Pension Gangster* before I sent the first draft to my publisher. You have both made the book better and I owe you both (massive) drinks.

Thank you to Will Dady at Renard Press for believing in this book before it was even written, and for such an enjoyable and collaborative approach to publishing.

The pictures of KitKats and quizzes in *Pension Gangster* were drawn by Beth Bridger who owns the organic clothing company *Boodle* – clothes which I am usually wearing and that you should check out. I don't think she has a KitKat top though... yet.

And finally, Indy, I'm sorry this probably isn't the non-fiction book you were hoping for, but the truth is, I don't know much about elephants or football. But hey, you're clearly the boss, so what shall I write next, kiddo?

ABOUT THE AUTHOR

Alongside his career in finance, Tim Ewins performed stand-up comedy for eight years. He also had a very brief acting stint (he's in the film *Bronson*, somewhere in the background) before turning to writing. His first novel, *We Are Animals*, was published in 2021, followed by *Tiny Pieces of Enid* in 2023. *Pension Gangster* is his first non-fiction book. When not writing, Tim enjoys learning about football through his eager son, reading (of course), swimming and spending time at home in Clevedon with his wife and son.

If you have any questions or feedback, you can contact Tim via his website:

TIM-EWINS.COM/CONTACT

A NOTE ON SUSTAINABILITY

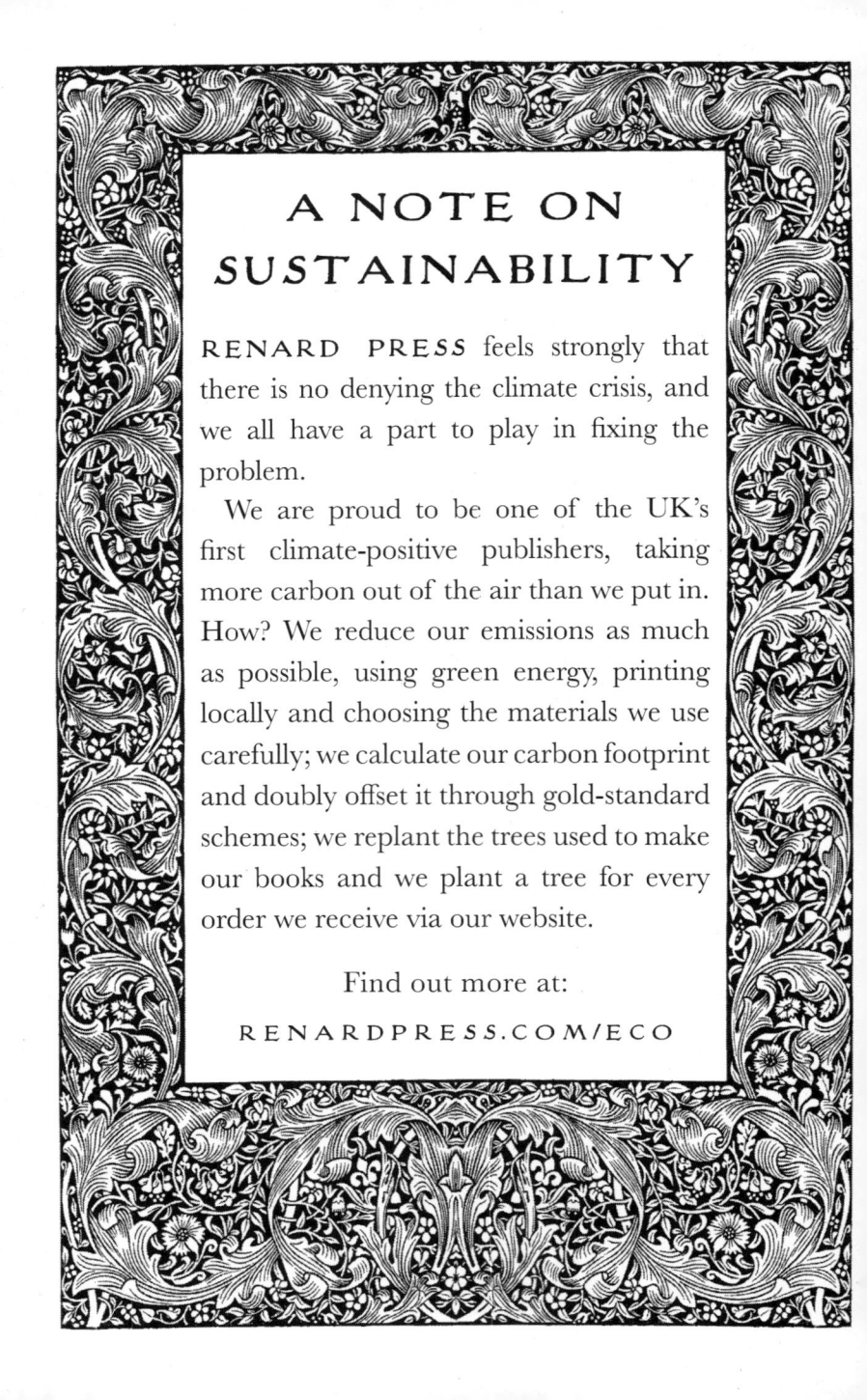

RENARD PRESS feels strongly that there is no denying the climate crisis, and we all have a part to play in fixing the problem.

We are proud to be one of the UK's first climate-positive publishers, taking more carbon out of the air than we put in. How? We reduce our emissions as much as possible, using green energy, printing locally and choosing the materials we use carefully; we calculate our carbon footprint and doubly offset it through gold-standard schemes; we replant the trees used to make our books and we plant a tree for every order we receive via our website.

Find out more at:
RENARDPRESS.COM/ECO